Cape Town

Footprint

Francisca Kellett

Contents

Listings

See inside back cover for Around Cape Town map

About the author

Francisca Kellett first visited Africa as an anthropology student in the mid-1990s, and has since found it hard to stay away. She has travelled extensively in southern and eastern Africa, straying occasionally as far as Egypt and Morocco, although South Africa remains her preferred port of call. A journalist and photographer, Francisca has contributed to a number of guidebooks, newspapers, travel magazines and websites. She also specializes in development issues and writes political and environmental reviews for African news magazines. As well as being the author of this pocket handbook she is also a contributor of the *South Africa Handbook*. When not in Africa, she lives in the rather less exotic location of North London.

Cape Town is a city worth crossing the world for. First impressions simply don't get any better – the city is dominated by the golden splendour of Table Mountain, its steep slopes and flat top towering between the wild shores of the Atlantic. It is a city that is at once intense and laid back. The severity of the mountain is tempered by the soft, white sand of its beaches, the grand pomposity of its colonial buildings mollified by the buzzing markets that surround them. Its very nature seems audaciously fickle, evoking bafflingly conflicting images – notorious Robben Island and the body-beautiful hedonism of Clifton Beach, the call of the muezzin from the Bo-Kaap mosques mingling with the beats of funk and house in cool bars, the bronzed beach babe who drives in an open-top sports car past homeless, street-side families, opulent wine estates and the shanty towns of the Cape Flats. All of these images, however strange, are real and jostle for attention.

Collective charisma

The main thing that will grab your attention though is the people. Cape Town's population has an even greater collective charisma than Table Mountain, a mix of cultures, religions and ethnicities that drive the pulse of the city. Known as the 'Mother City' of South Africa, its uneasy past – seat of colonial rule, platform of apartheid and hotbed of political struggle – has done little to quench the communal vivacity that is so palpable in Cape Town today. The fabric of the city is undeniably energetic, from the waves that pound the shoreline to the countless festivals that fill the streets, yet Capetonians are renowned for their nonchalant attitude and come-what-may approach. This is the source of much contention for the rest of South Africa, which seems to fluctuate between despising Cape Town for its blasé and careless approach and applauding it for the very lifestyle that creates such an outlook. In typical Cape Town fashion, people seem little bothered by what outsiders think, content instead to bask in the reflected splendour of their city.

Cape capers

And who could blame them. This bewildering mix of environments and communities makes Cape Town an instantly likeable and captivating place. Around the city are some of the South Africa's highlights, from the stunning natural beauty and historical Cape Dutch wine estates of the Winelands, to the pretty seaside resorts and superb whale watching of the Whale Coast. Few places in the world can offer mountain hiking and lazing on a beach in one morning, and tasting world-class wines or drinking home-brewed beer in a township *shebeen* in the evening. No big deal, you'll soon be thinking – just like a Capetonian.

At a glance

The city centre

The heart of Cape Town lies in a 'bowl' formed by a horseshoe of mountains – Signal Hill, Table Mountain and Devil's Peak – rolling down to the Atlantic. Cradled between the slopes and the sea lies the central business district, a compact grid of broad streets lined with a hotch-potch of modern high-rises and colonial buildings. Adderley Street is the main artery of the commercial centre, busy with a constant throng of shoppers, but at its southern end it turns into quiet, tree-lined Government Avenue which holds the city's major museums and historical buildings. A few blocks west lies quirky Long Street, backpacker central and a hive of trendy restaurants and late-night bars. Behind the centre, rolling up the southern slopes of the City Bowl, are the historical inner-city suburbs of Gardens, Oranjezicht and Tamboerskloof, affluent and leafy districts dominated by Table Mountain. To the west, on the slopes of Signal Hill, are the altogether different, but no less picturesque cobbled streets of the Bo-Kaap, the historical Muslim area which somehow survived apartheid's bulldozers.

Victoria and Alfred Waterfront

Northwest of the City Bowl lies Cape Town's original Victorian harbour, the city's most popular attraction. The whole area was completely renovated in the early 1990s, and today original buildings stand shoulder to shoulder with mock-Victorian shopping centres, al fresco restaurants and cinemas, all crowding along a waterside walkway with Table Mountain looming in the background. It is an enjoyable area, but very touristy – prices are higher in restaurants and shops, and some say over-sanitized and artificial. Recent developments, however, such as the opening of the Nelson Mandela Gateway to nearby Robben Island, have gone some way in raising the area's profile.

Atlantic Seaboard

Along the shore from the V & A Waterfront lies the modern
residential area of Green Point, a bland throng of apartment blocks
crowding between Signal Hill and the rocky shoreline, but hiding
a huddle of colourful Victorian bungalows, part of the Bo-Kaap.
This has become Cape Town's major gay and lesbian hub, and the
city's wildest bars and clubs stretch along the main Somerset Road.
Following this road away from the City Bowl leads to Sea Point, a
similarly modern coastal district with a sizeable Jewish population.
In contrast to Green Point however, Sea Point has a real family
atmosphere and during the summer feels more like a European
seaside resort than a South African suburb. Clifton, further round
the peninsula from Sea Point, is Cape Town's Beverley Hills (-on
-Sea, if you like). This is where the rich and beautiful come to see
and be seen, to show off bikinis and yachts, flex muscles and bask.
Made up of a string of rocky coves, the small, white sand beaches
are beautiful, backed by some of Cape Town's most sought-after
villas and apartments, but surprisingly there is little in the way of
nightlife or restaurants here. Camps Bay, just round the headland,
has the monopoly on these. The main road stretching behind the
long, more family-oriented beach is lined with some of the best
seafood restaurants and 'sundowner' bars in Cape Town.

Southern Suburbs

On the other side of the City Bowl, stretching southeast along the
slopes of Devil's Peak towards False Bay, are Cape Town's Southern
Suburbs. The first suburb, Woodstock, is mainly a working-class
coloured district, its rundown commercial centre hiding an attractive mesh of beautiful Victorian bungalows. Further along lies the
bohemian hub of Observatory, an appealing grid of brightly
painted houses, filled with trendy student-friendly bars, cafés and
restaurants. The next suburbs of Mowbray, Rosebank and
Rondebosch lie just below the University of Cape Town, getting pro-
gressively smarter (and whiter) as you progress round the mountain.

Claremont, on the other side of Table Mountain, leads to beautiful Constantia, Cape Town's wealthiest suburb. Behind here, stretching up the slopes of Table Mountain, are the Kirstenbosch Botanical Gardens, a perfect backdrop to the heavily fortified mansions.

Cape Flats

The majority of Cape Town's inhabitants live in the townships of the Cape Flats, the vast plain stretching between Table Mountain and the Winelands. This is the first area that visitors pass through on their way from the airport to the city centre, but it is rarely visited by tourists and steadfastly avoided by white Capetonians. At first glance, the townships do seem barren and bleak, but beyond the imposing light towers and wire fences lie well-established and thriving communities, holding much of Cape Town's contemporary culture. The main townships – Guguletu, Langa, Mitchell's Plain, Crossroads and Khayelitsha – remain largely either coloured or black, while poverty and crime are a continuing scourge. Yet their pivotal role in the struggle against apartheid secured their importance in the life of Cape Town, and a visit to the townships provides a far broader sense of what the city is all about.

False Bay

At the other end of the peninsula from the city centre is False Bay, a vast arch stretching from the Cape of Good Hope to the headland before Walker's Bay and Hermanus in the east. False Bay is defined by a string of small seaside towns and fishing villages, including delightful Kalk Bay, an artsy village with the bay's only coloured fishing community, and well-established Simon's Town, the most family-oriented beach area around Cape Town. Further south is famous Boulders Beach, with its entertaining colony of African penguins, and finally the Cape of Good Hope Nature Reserve, a superb vantage point and excellent hiking country.

★ **Ten of the best**

1 **Table Mountain** Take the cable car to the top and marvel at the spectacular views over the city, p45.

2 **Kirstenbosch Botanical Gardens** Stroll through the magnificent gardens and picnic in one of the most beautiful settings in South Africa, p72.

3 **Robben Island** Visit the notorious prison where Nelson Mandela was held for 18 years and learn about the struggles of political prisoners during apartheid, p57.

4 **Company's Gardens and Government Avenue** Wander through the beautiful gardens and leafy avenue in the heart of the city, lined with historical museums and colonial buildings, p33.

5 **District Six Museum** Visit Cape Town's finest museum, exploring the devastating effects of apartheid on local communities, p42.

6 **Cape of Good Hope Nature Reserve** Explore the rugged area of Cape Point and climb to the superb views of False Bay and the Atlantic, p64.

7 **Boulders Beach** Watch the colony of African penguins waddling and squabbling about their daily business at Boulders Beach, p83.

8 **Clifton** Bronze your limbs with the rich and beautiful at Cape Town's most exclusive beach, p60.

9 **Whale watching in Hermanus** Head to Hermanus, an hour from Cape Town, for some of the finest whale watching in the world, p106.

10 **Winelands** Spend a day touring the beautiful valleys of the Winelands, trying South Africa's best wines at historical estates, p88.

Trip planner

It would take months to take in everything Cape Town and its surroundings have to offer, but a week is enough to get a taster. On an exposed peninsula between two oceans, Cape Town's weather is notoriously fickle. The winter months are cool and wet, but most weeks will have at least one day of bright sunshine. In summer temperatures can get well above 30°C, with perfect blue skies and cooling breezes, but this can change, with little warning, to fierce winds, horizontal rain and wild seas. Be prepared, therefore, to change your plans at the last minute.

Day one
A wonderful start and the best place to get a grip of Cape Town's layout is from the top of Table Mountain. A cable car whisks visitors to the summit offering amazing views. From here, head back down and take a taxi to Government Avenue. This delightful oak-shaded pedestrian road takes you past Company's Garden, some of the city's finest museums and colonial buildings. Head east to the superb District Six Museum, or wander towards Greenmarket Square.

Day two
The Victoria and Alfred Waterfront is a tourist-friendly development packed with shops, bars and restaurants and has an excellent aquarium. You can observe seals cavorting in the water and buskers entertaining diners, while watching the everyday life of a working harbour. The Nelson Mandela Gateway is here too, where you catch the ferry to Robben Island. Tours take three hours and provide an insight to the Machiavellian workings of the apartheid system.

Day three
To explore the great outdoors, take a drive to Cape of Good Hope, a beautifully wild area offering panoramic views and good walks as well as a couple of wild beaches perfect for a picnic. Drive back

along the False Bay Seaboard and stop off at Boulders Beach, a haven for a huge colony of African penguins. They are amazingly nonchalant about humans, and you can get very close and watch them waddling about their business.

Day four
Spend half a day exploring the Southern Suburbs which stretch around Table Mountain. The obvious highlight is the Kirstenbosch Botanical Gardens. They are amongst the finest in the world and stunning, not least due to their setting, creeping up the slopes of Table Mountain. Similarly beautiful is the wealthy area of Constantia with its lush setting and excellent vineyards. In sharp contrast are the nearby Cape Flats, an enormous spread of townships and shantytowns. They are best visited on a tour which takes half a day.

Day five
The Whale Coast is a true highlight during the late winter and spring months, when huge numbers of Southern Right whales come into the bays to calve. Hermanus, just an hour from Cape Town, is hailed as having the best land-based whale watching in the world. You could come here for a day trip, but it is a pleasant spot to spend a night by the sea.

Day six
Spend a lazy day at one of the beaches on the Atlantic Seaboard. These are some of the most beautiful in the world – perfect arches of white sand fringed by turquoise water. Camps Bay and Clifton have the added advantage of being frequented by Cape Town's movers and shakers, making them perfect for a few hours of people watching. Alternatively, drive around the mountain to False Bay, with its pretty towns, child-friendly beaches and warm waters. Both seaboards have an excellent choice of seafood restaurants, perfect for a large, end-of-holiday meal.

Contemporary Cape Town

Cape Town is an unquenchably optimistic city. Although still recovering from decades of white minority rule, Capetonians have an unwavering belief in a bright and promising future. This upbeat and easygoing nature has long defined the city. Locals are noticeably friendlier and more laidback than in other parts of the country, and the streets and markets buzz with a confident energy. But it is its exceptionally varied population that distinguishes Cape Town first and foremost – the term 'Rainbow Nation' seems more appropriate here than elsewhere.

Certainly, Cape Town's population is the most cosmopolitan in the country. It has a comparatively small black African population – about a third of the total – while the distinctive 'Cape coloured' community makes up over half of the population. These are descendents of slaves brought from India, East Africa and Madagascar who interacted with European and local indigenous people, and today comprise much of the city's middle class. The third largest group is made up of white descendents of Dutch and British settlers, but there is also a sizeable Asian community.

Whatever their origins, Capetonians are fiercely proud of their city, and go about life with a certain boisterousness that is both sneered at and envied by the rest of South Africa's urban population. A long-standing rivalry remains between Johannesburg and Cape Town – a sort of New York/LA thing, where Capetonians are jealous of Jo'burg's strong economy, and Jo'burg residents crave Cape Town's location and relaxed way of life. While Jo'burg's population is seen as sophisticated but fundamentally dull, Capetonians are perceived as hungover hippies who spend far too much time lazing around on beaches. The fact that Cape Town is invaded every summer by tens of thousands of Jo'burg residents, however, seems to say a lot.

Jealousies aside, much of Cape Town's character has been sculpted by its rich diversity of languages. Afrikaans and English are most commonly heard, although the increasing black population is bringing Xhosa to the forefront. Afrikaans is the main language of Cape Town's coloured population, as well as being a major player in the identity of white Afrikaners. Although there are fewer of the latter in Cape Town than in other parts of the country, the Winelands is a major focal point of Afrikaner culture. Their distinctive Cape Dutch architecture, at its best on the historical wine estates around Stellenbosch and Paarl, remains the most celebrated in South Africa. In origins Afrikaans is a creolized version of Dutch – the result of the interaction between Cape Town's slave and colonial cultures. In the townships of the Cape Flats, Afrikaans is spoken with a dialect known as *Kapie Taal*, with English and Xhosa words thrown in to produce a distinctive combination which is evolving fast into a new language. The Cape Flats are in fact a veritable hotbed of new developments in the life of the city. Music is a major focal point everywhere in Cape Town, but much of it originates here, particularly distinctive Cape Jazz.

Religion is similarly varied, with strong Christian, Muslim and Jewish communities, as well as those following African traditions. Perhaps the best-known of Cape Town's religious groups is known as the Cape Malays, the Muslim community focused on the Bo-Kaap. The term Cape Malay, however, is a misnomer – in reality a very small percentage of the population originated in Malaysia. Islam was instead introduced from India, Indonesia and East Africa, from slaves and political dissidents introduced by the Dutch East India Company in the 16th and 17th centuries. Today, the Muslim community retains a strong identity which does much to define Cape Town's diverse religious scene. Nevertheless, despite the rich mix of cultures that makes up the city's population, many still identify themselves by, and live according to, race.

Such sentiments remain largely an issue of geography and economics. The Group Areas Act of the 1960s ensured that all prime land was in white hands – districts in the centre of town, by the seaside or along the lush slopes of Table Mountain, while coloured and black communities were, often forcibly, resettled in townships on the bleak and barren Cape Flats. This devastating urban planning of apartheid segregated all residential areas by race. The official colour barriers may have long since disappeared and residential boundaries are shifting, but districts are by and large still defined by colour. This can mean that the visitor gains a lopsided view of Cape Town – experiencing the ordered, affluent city that barely hints at the grinding poverty found in less visible parts.

Economics, too, play a crucial role. The division between rich and poor remains – put simply, the most affluent sector is white and the poorest black. Thankfully, this is changing: a black middle class has emerged in recent years, and the coloured middle class is strengthening. Certainly, Cape Town is keen to shift thoughts regarding race and colour. The term coloured, for example, has been rejected by some as inappropriate in a post-apartheid South Africa. Others have proudly reclaimed it as a symbol of their distinct culture and history.

However people define themselves, Capetonians seem unanimous in their pride in their city. Apartheid's hangover is still evident, but there seems to be an ever-strengthening sense of celebration of Cape Town's many different sides, a move towards rejoicing over cultural differences rather than airbrushing them out. Far from the spaced out, dippy image that Cape Town suffers in other South African cities, it seems critically aware of what drives it – and it is this that makes it what it is.

There are frequent direct flights to Cape Town from most European countries, the United States, Australia and neighbouring African states. The cost of a ticket can be expensive – the city is becoming more and more popular, and prices can be correspondingly high. Booking as far in advance as possible, however, can bring prices down considerably.

Cape Town sadly lacks a decent public transport system. Thankfully, most of the city's oldest buildings, museums, galleries and the commercial centre are concentrated in a relatively small area. There is a bus network which travels between the city centre and the Southern Suburbs, but it can be slow and tiring. Faster and more efficient are the minibus taxis which are generally safe to use. Taxis are affordable, but can be hard to organize, although the local rikki taxis can be very good value for the major sights and backpacker lodges. To get the most out of the city and to visit the suburbs, beaches, Winelands and Whale Coast, it's a good idea to rent a car.

Getting there

Air

From Europe Although Europe to Cape Town flights are long haul, they are surprisingly easy. Flights usually last about 12 to 13 hours, and are always overnight, but the main advantage is that there is no jetlag – the time difference is only +2 GMT. **British Airways** and **South African Airways** are the two main flight operators, but all of the major European carriers serve Cape Town (usually via other cities, such as Amsterdam or Frankfurt), often at very competitive prices. During peak season, a direct return flight can cost as much as £1,200, but if you book several months in advance, this can drop to below £500. Prices drop further if you choose an indirect flight. European carriers such as **Lufthansa** and **KLM** often have good value offers with return flights from £450, although these travel via another European city and often stop off at Johannesburg. At time of writing, **Virgin Atlantic** was offering competitive flights to Johannesburg, with cheap onward connections to Cape Town.

From North America **South African Airways** runs flights from JFK New York to Johannesburg, with onward connections to Cape Town four times a week (Tuesday, Friday, Saturday and Sunday at time of writing). Flight time is around 17 hours, with prices usually around the £800 mark. There are also several weekly flights from Atlanta and Miami. **American Airlines** has a code-sharing agreement with *British Airways*, making it possible to fly from major US airports to Cape Town via London. Prices start at £700, and the flight time is about 19 hours in total, although stop-over time in London can be up to 12 hours. **Delta Airlines** has a more convenient agreement with *South African Airways*, with daily non-stop flights between JFK New York and Johannesburg, with onward connections to Cape Town. Alternatively, there is a daily flight from JFK to Cape Town via Atlanta. Fares vary widely, but are usually in the range of £700-1400, and the flight time is around 17 hours.

From Australia and New Zealand **Qantas** runs flights from Sydney and Perth to Johannesburg, with onward connections to Cape Town. Flights run four times a week (Monday, Thursday, Saturday and Sunday at time of writing), and prices start at about £600, although they can be double this during peak season. Flight time is around 11 hours. **South African Airways** also has four weekly flights from Perth to Johannesburg – prices are similar. Travellers from New Zealand will have to travel via Australia as there are no direct flights to South Africa from Auckland.

Airport information Cape Town International Airport is a modern airport with convenient shops, car rental and travel agents desks.

 Airlines and agents

American Airlines, T 1800-4337300, www.aa.com
British Airways, T 0845-7733377 www.britishairways.com
Delta Airlines, T 1800-2414141, www.delta.com
KLM, T 0870-5074047, www.klm.com
Lufthansa, T 0845-7737747, www.lufthansa.com
Qantas, T 0845-7747767, www.qantas.com
South African Airways, T +27115752480, T 0870-7471111
www.flysaa.com
Virgin Atlantic, T 1800-8628621, www.virgin-atlantic.com

Websites
www.cheapflights.com
www.expedia.com
www.flynow.com
www.istc.org
www.statravel.com
www.travelocity.com

International long haul flights are always overnight, which means they arrive at a reasonable time in the morning. The International and Domestic terminals are a 20-minute drive from the city centre, a 22-km trip. Expect to pay up to R250 for a taxi to the centre of town – they should have a special airport licence and must use their meter by law. It is better value to get one of the shuttle buses that operate the route. Airport Shuttle Service is good value for more than one as rates vary according to the number using it. The service extends as far as Simon's Town and Kommetjie, with a minimum charge of R40. Backpackers Shuttle is also convenient and good value running from the airport to central hostels.

Getting around

Bus
A good service, the Waterfront bus, with a distinctive blue wave pattern on the side, runs from Cape Town railway station to the Victoria and Alfred Waterfront. It runs every 15 minutes. Generally though services are slow and not worth taking.

Car
People drive fast and overtaking on blind corners is the norm. Although drink driving carries heavy penalties, it remains common-place, so it's best not to drive at night – stick to taxis. Parking is generally not a problem. Most of the city centre has demarcated areas for parking, costing about R4 per hour. You either need to buy a R30 card (from newsagents) or hand over coins to official parking attendants (in blue uniforms). Petrol prices have been increasing somewhat lately, but remain relatively good value compared to Europe. There are plenty of large petrol stations around the city, but note that none are self-service and you must pay in cash. At quiet times car hire prices should be considerably cheaper than around December and January. The cheapest local

car hire companies change frequently – it's a good idea to check at backpacker hostels to see which ones they recommend.

Cycling

Despite Cape Town's outdoorsy vibe, suprisingly few people get about by bicycle. There are few cycle lanes in the city and the frenetic driving of many motorists can make it unsafe. Futhermore, most of the main sites are within easy walking distance of each other. However, cycling as a sport is very popular and mountain biking in particular has taken on in a big way. In March, Cape Town is host to the world's largest timed cycle race, a mamoth trail skirting around False Bay and over the mountains to the city. Much of the area around Cape Town is very well suited to mountain biking, with good trails around Table Mountain as well as several popular routes criss-crossing the Winelands. See Sports, p203, for details of companies that provide bike hire and organize mountain biking trips.

Minibus taxis

These serve all areas of the city on fixed routes, and leave from the minibus terminal accessed from the top floor of the Sanlam Golden Acre shopping centre on Adderley Street. They can also be flagged down from the street. Minibuses to the Atlantic coast usually leave from outside *OK Bazaars* on Adderley Street. Most trips cost R2.50-3. They stop running at 1900. Unlike in some South African cities, these are generally safe to use, although avoid anywhere outside of the city centre, do your best not to look like a tourist and leave all valuables at home. See Directory, p223.

Rikki taxis

These small shared people-carriers are a cheaper alternative to getting around the city. You need to call one, but they pick up several people along the route, bringing down costs. See Directory, p223.

Travel extras

Money
The South African currency is the Rand (R) which is divided into 100 cents (c). As long as you have the right type of card and sufficient funds, using an ATM (Automatic Teller Machine) is the most convenient and cheapest way of obtaining funds.

Safety
Cape Town has had problems of crime directed at tourists in the past, but this has improved significantly in recent years. Many of the problem areas now have CCTV cameras in the streets, and private security guards protect shops, restaurants and hotels. The most simple points to remember are: avoid carrying valuables and conceal cameras; don't walk around areas you're not familiar with; try not to look like a tourist; don't walk anywhere other than the busiest areas late at night; and make sure you do not drive in rural areas after dark. If you are going to be travelling alone in a car, it's advisable to take your mobile phone or hire one.

Tipping
Waiters, hotel porters, stewards, chambermaids and tour guides will expect a tip – 10-15% is an acceptable average.

Vaccinations
South Africa requires yellow fever vaccination certificates from travellers who have entered from other (especially Central and West African, countries. There is no malaria in the Western Cape.

Visas
All visitors are issued with a 90-day tourist visa.

Taxis

There are several ranks dotted around town – the most useful ones are outside the train station at Adderley Street, by the Holiday Inn on Greenmarket Square, and on Long Street. You can also flag down any that you see cruising around. If you are outside the city centre, you will have to call one in advance. Be sure to get a quote as prices can vary a lot. See Directory, p223, for details of taxi firms.

Train/metro

Metrorail serve the suburbs. Services run as far as Simon's Town, but also go out as far as Worcester. We have received conflicting reports as to how safe these trains are. It is probably safest to use the trains at peak times when all carriages and classes are busy.

Walking

Thankfully, most of the city's oldest buildings, museums, galleries and the commercial centre are concentrated in a relatively small area and best explored on foot. Most of the key sites are an easy stroll from each other – Long Street, Government Avenue, Adderley Street, Greenmarket Square and the Castle of Good Hope are all within a 20-minute radius. The V & A Waterfront is a bit of a walk away, and really only accessible by car, bus, or on the soon to be completed canal. Similarly, the beaches, suburbs and the Cape of Good Hope are all inaccessible by foot. Best bet is to hire a car.

Tours

City centre tours

Cape Town Tourism owns the Explorer Bus, a double- decker top-less bus which follows a two-hour route around the city. Contact the main tourist office for details, T 021-4264260. *Elwierda Topless Tours*, T 021-4185888, also organizes a two-hour city tour. Buses depart hourly between 0940 and 1440, starting from the Waterfront.

Cultural tours

Grassroute Tours, T 021-7061006, www.grassroutetours.com, specializes in township tours beginning in District Six and continuing to Langa and Khayelitsha, also a history of Cape Muslims tour. This company works with the communities it visits, putting back some of the proceeds. Half-day tours cost around R225. *Western Cape Action Tours*, T 021-4611371, wcat@iafrica.com Township tours with a strong focus on political issues, with visits to historically significant sights, discussions are encouraged, tours are led by people who took part in the liberation struggle. More thought- provoking and less voyeuristic than most other tours. Half-day tours R180. Recommended. *Tana-Baru Tours*, T 021-4240719, conduct specialist tours of the Cape Malay Quarter lasting two hours. Led by Shereen Habih, they are interesting and good value, about R80 per person. Also offer township tours lasting three hours and costing from R250. *Roots Africa Tours*, T 021-9878330, www.rootsafrica.co.za, Khayelitsha Township tours, Winelands, Robben Island trips.

Boat tours

Condor Charters, T 021-4191780, offer harbour tours in a luxury motor yacht, fully equipped for private parties, leaves from Quay 4. *Spirit of Victoria*, T 021-4191780, a 58-foot Graff rigged Schooner, a stylish way to explore the harbour and the bay, German and French spoken. *Tigresse Cruises*, T 021-4241455, have daily departures from the Waterfront, sunset cruises and day trips in a fine modern sailing boat, booking advised during peak periods. *Waterfront Charters*, Quay 5, V & A Waterfront, T 021-4180134, sales@waterfront charters.co.za, offers a variety of boat trips in and around the harbour. Champagne sunset cruise every evening, duration 1½ hours. *Spirit of Just Nuisance*, T 082-7375263 or T 083-2577760 offer tours around the Cape of Good Hope including short trips around the harbour area including a special visit to the naval dockyard. The boat departs approximately every 45 minutes from the pier by the Quayside Centre in Simon's Town.

Expect to pay R20 for adults, R10 for children. Recommended if you only have a limited amount of time to spend in Simon's Town. They also organize trips to Seal Island and fishing trips – call ahead to check times. *SV Curlew*, T 021-7861226 or T 082-2243909, highgables@iafrica.com, is a traditional sailing vessel that can carry up to 25 passengers. Cruises around the Cape of Good Hope and and sunset cruises by appointment. *Sweet Sunshine*, T 082-5755655, is a 42-foot motorized sailing catamaran, offering a variety of cruises including a four-hour trip around Cape Point, trips to Seal Island and sunset cruises. Outings and trips towards whales (during the season, July-November), depart from the pier by the Quayside Centre, Simon's Town.

Coach tours

Elwierda Tours, T 021-4185888. Full-day tours to Cape Point and peninsula tours. *Hylton Ross*, T 021-5111784, www.hyltonross.co.za offer full- and half-day tours to Cape Point, historic city tours, Winelands tours. *Mother City Tours*, T 021-4483817, F 4483844, have full- and half-day peninsula tours. *Easy Rider Wine Tours*, T 021-8864651, stumble@iafrica.com, offer the hugely popular Stellenbosch wine tour organized by the *Stumble Inn*. Tours take in five estates, with tastings in each, lunch and cheese tasting included, good value although they tend to be crowded and chaotic.

Whale Coast tours

Coastal Kayak Trails, T 021-3410405, offer various routes and guided kayak tours. *Dyer Island Cruises*, T 021-3841266, take punters on boat trips to Dyer Island. *Southern Right Charters*, T 082-3530550, are a boat-based whale watching company. *Walker Bay Adventures*, just out of town towards Gansbaai at Prawn Flats, T 021-3140925, kwanzyl@netdial.co.za, hire out all types of boats, canoes, rowing boats, pedaloes, plus fishing equipment. Daily cruises on the lagoon, weather permitting, for larger groups. The ever-popular sundowner cruise is also on offer.

Tourist information

Cape Town Tourism, The Pinnacle, corner of Burg and Castle sts, T 021-4264260, F 4264266, www.cape-town.org *Open Mon-Fri, 0800-1900, Sat, 0830-1400 and Sun, 0900-1300.* The main, official city tourist office and can help with bookings and tours throughout the Western Cape. It is an excellent source of information and a good first stop in the city. In addition to providing practical information about Cape Town, it can help with accommodation bookings and visiting other provinces, and has a good café and internet access.

Victoria and Alfred Waterfront, Clock Tower centre, open daily, *0900-1800, T 021-4054500, www.waterfront.co.za* There is a brand new tourist information centre at the Waterfront. As well as handing out maps and leaflets on the area, you can also book flights, tours, car rental, check your email and have a coffee overlooking the harbour.

 Township tourism

A popular new tourism initiative in the city has been 'Township Tourism', where houses (and in some cases shacks) in the townships of the Cape Flats have been opened to tourists. While this allows visitors to experience this lesser-seen side of Cape Town and get a feel for township life, it also provides much needed tourist dollars in underprivileged areas. One of the best places to stay for a night or two is Vicky's B&B, T 082-2252986 (mob), or vickysbandb@yahoo.com, in Khayelitsha, run by the welcoming Vicky. Her self-built house has two simple, clean double rooms, and she cooks excellent meals and can organize visits to local schools and nights out in the nearby *shebeen*.

Western Cape Tourism Board, PO Box 3878, Tyger Valley, 7536, T 021-9144613, F 9144610, wctbcape@iafrica.com, www.cape tourism.co.za   This office provides tourist information on the Cape outside of Cape Town.

For the **Wine Routes** you can also get in touch with Stellenbosch Wine Route Office, T 021-8864310, www.wineroute.co.za   *Open Mon-Fri 0830-1300, 1400-1700*. Paarl Wine Route, T 021-8723605, www.paarlwine.co.za   Plenty of information from how to get around to accommodation and eating.

Hermanus Tourism Bureau, Old Station Building, Mitchell Street, T 028-3122629, F 3130305, www.hermanus.co.za   *Open from Mon-Sat 0900-1700. Sun 0900-1200 from May-Jul and 0900-1400 from Aug-Apr.* Aside from helping you find suitable accommodation, the office can arrange guided walks in and around town.

Table Mountain 31 The mountain makes Cape Town the city that it is.

The city centre 32 A mish-mash of modern high-rises, beautiful colonial buildings, African stylie markets, peaceful gardens and museums aplenty.

Victoria and Alfred Waterfront 53 Full to the brim with restaurants, bars and shops, it is also home to the impressive aquarium and the Nelson Mandela Gateway to nearby Robben Island.

Atlantic Seaboard 59 This is the peninsula's most spectacular stretch of coast with the Twelve Apostles providing the backdrop. Each town has its own character from body-beautiful hedonism to seaside family resort.

Southern Suburbs 68 Once the enclave of affluent whites, today there is an interesting mix of people and two of Cape Town's finest attractions, Kirstenbosch Botanical Gardens and Constantia.

False Bay 74 The bay is a string of seaside resorts and fishing villages that have a distinct family feel. A bit twee but the droves of penguins and chance of seeing whales compensates.

★ Table Mountain

Cape Town is defined, first and foremost, by Table Mountain. The centre of the city nestles beneath it, and it seems almost rude not to make it your first stop. Being whisked to the summit by cable car and taking in the spectacular views is without doubt a highlight, and an excellent introduction to the layout of the city and the astounding variety of environments found on the peninsula.

T 021-4248181, www.tablemountain.co.za *0830-2100 (1930 in winter). R85 for a return, discounts for children. Latest mountain weather reports, T021-4245148. The tourist office shuttle bus to the Lower Cable Car leaves every half hour from the main office on Burg St. Taxis cost R50-60 from the city centre. Map 1, C3, p246*

Rising a sheer 1,073 m from the coastal plain, the mountain dominates almost every view of the city, its sharp slopes and level top making it one of the world's best-known city backdrops. For centuries, it was the first sight of Cape Town afforded to seafarers, its looming presence visible for hundreds of kilometres. Certainly, its size continues to astonish visitors today, but it is the mountain's wilderness, bang in the middle of a bustling conurbation, that makes the biggest impression. Table Mountain sustains over 1,400 species of flora, as well as baboons, dassies (large rodents) and countless birds. Watch out for the 'Table Cloth', the impressive layer of cloud that descends on the top of the mountain most afternoons, its edges wafting down the highest slopes.

It is worth going to the top for the dizzying trip in the cable car alone. Built in 1997 the two cars, each carrying up to 65 passengers, with the floor rotating, allow for a full 360 degree view. The average journey time is three minutes. There is a bistro restaurant and souvenir shop at the top station, as well as a cheaper café. From here, a range of paths wind across the rocky top, each leading to different viewpoints over the peninsula.

Much of the area is a nature reserve, and the mountain itself is protected as a national monument. For many years there were only a few known paths to the top, but today there are an estimated 500. One of the easier popular routes starts from Kirstenbosch Botanical Gardens and takes about three hours to get to the top. However, even busy routes should not be taken lightly. Given Table Mountain's size and location, conditions can change alarmingly quickly. The weather may seem clear and calm when you set out, but fog and rain can descend without warning. The mountain has claimed its fair share of lives. Before venturing out, ensure that you have suitable clothing, food and water. Inexperienced hikers, or those interested in learning more about the mountain's flora and fauna, should take a guide or a walking tour.

● *Lion's Head is an easier, alternative climb offering stunning 360 degree views. It takes two hours and is popular at full moon to watch the sunset and descend by the light of the moon. Signal Hill, further along, is accessible by car and has equally spectacular views.*

The city centre

The city itself rolls from the lower slopes of Table Mountain and holds most of Cape Town's major sights and attractions. From the Lower Cableway Station, you look out over **City Bowl***, the central residential suburbs of Tamboerskloof, Gardens, Oranjezicht and Vredehoek, and beyond here lie the high-rise blocks of the business district.*

*Closest to the mountain is **Oranjezicht**, a quiet district with a good selection of places to stay. **Vredehoek**, on the other hand, has mostly been given over to ugly high-rise apartments. **Gardens** is a lively neighbourhood with a good choice of restaurants and guesthouses. Cape Town's best-known hotel, Mount Nelson, is situated here.*

*From here the land slopes gently towards the Waterfront, with the commercial heart of the city laid out in between. From the magnificent tree-lined **Government Avenue** and the oasis calm of **Company's** Gardens, the city opens up into a lively hub of broad streets buzzing with a medley of besuited executives, trendy media types and boisterous market sellers. This is the historical heart of the city, but also the commercial centre, and as such is a mish-mash of beautiful colonial buildings, modern office blocks and crowded shopping centres. **Adderley Street** is the main artery, with most sights a few blocks away. The superb **District Six Museum** and the **Castle of Good Hope** are a few blocks to the east; **Long Street**, the playground of the young and hip is a short stroll west, with the lively market at **Greenmarket Square** lying between.*

▶▶ *See Sleeping p113, Eating and drinking p135, Bars and clubs p165*

 Sights

Company's Garden
Free. Map 2, B7/C7, p249

Running alongside Government Avenue is the peaceful Company's Garden, situated on the site of Jan van Riebeeck's original vegetable garden, which was created in 1652 to grow produce for settlers and ships bound for the East, see p48. It is now a small botanical garden, with lawns, a variety of labelled trees and ponds filled with Japanese koi. The grey squirrels living amongst the oak trees were introduced by Cecil Rhodes – Cape Prime Minister from 1890-96 – from America. There are also a couple of statues here: opposite the

South African Public Library at the lower end of the garden, is the oldest statue in Cape Town, that of Sir George Grey, Governor of the Cape from 1854-62. Close by is a statue of Cecil Rhodes, pointing northwards, with an inscription reading, "Your hinterland is there", a reminder of his ambition to paint the map pink from the Cape to Cairo. There is a pleasant café in the garden, serving drinks and snacks beneath the trees.

South Africa Museum and Planetarium
Company's Garden, **T** 021-4243330, www.museums.org.za/sam/ *1000-1700. R8, children free. Free on Wed. Planetarium shows, Mon-Fri 1400, Sat/Sun, 1300, 1430. R10.* Map 2, C6, p248 See also Kids, p215

One of the city's most established museums, it specializes in natural history, ethnography and archaeology and is a good place to bring kids. The first part of the collection has some interesting displays depicting the pre-European history of southern Africa. In the Stone Age room is the Linton panel, a beautifully preserved example of San rock art representing what has been interpreted as trance experiments. The ethnographic galleries offer excellent displays on the San, Khoi and Xhosa, amongst others. There is also a small display of pieces recovered from Great Zimbabwe which illustrate what an important trade centre it was: cornelian beads from Cambay, India and Syrian glass from the 14th century. At the Planetarium next door presentations change every few months, but a view of the current night sky is shown on the first weekend of each month. The shows are fascinating and last an hour.

Bertram House
Government Av, **T** 021-4249381. *Tue-Sat, 0930-1630. R5.* Map 2, D6, p248

This early 19th-century red brick Georgian house has a distinctly English feel to it. The building houses a collection of porcelain, jewellery and English furniture, the majority bequeathed by Ann Lidderdale, a Capetonian and important civic figure in the city in the 1950s. It was her desire to establish a house museum to commemorate the British contribution to life at the Cape. It opened in 1984. Downstairs the two drawing rooms contain all the trappings of a bygone elegant age – card tables, a Hepplewhite settee, a square piano and a fine harp. Three rooms have wallpaper from London, a very expensive luxury for the period. Upstairs the Doris Tothill silver tea set and the hair jewellery are particularly fine. There is a café set in the gardens.

Jewish Museum

Paddock Av, **T** 021-4651546, www.sajewishmuseum.co.za *Sun-Thu 1000-1700, Fri 1000-1400. R30, R10 for kids. Map 2, D7, p249*

In 1841 a congregation of 17 men assembled for the first time in Cape Town to celebrate Yom Kippur. At the meeting they set about the task of raising funds to build a synagogue, and in 1862 the foundation stone was laid for the first synagogue in southern Africa. The following year the building was completed and furnished – quite a feat for such a small community at the time. Inside the newly-renovated museum is a rich and rare collection of items depicting the history of the Cape Town Hebrew Congregation and other congregations in the Cape Province. On display upstairs are bronze Sabbath oil lamps, *Chanukkah* lamps, *Bessamin* spice containers, *Torah* scrolls, *Kiddush* cups and candlesticks. There is a beautiful stained-glass window depicting the Ten Commandments in Hebrew. From here a glass corridor leads you to a new section of the museum which is devoted to the history of Jewish immigration to the Cape, mainly from Lithuania. A lot of thought has been put into the displays, which include photographs, immigration certificates, videos and a full reconstruction of a Lithuanian *shetl* or village. The museum complex also houses a library, café and bookshop.

Aerial view of city from Signal Hill
Despite Cape Town's laid back, beach bum image, the central business district is another example of the city's diversity

Holocaust Centre

Paddock Av, **T** 021-4625554, www.museums.org.za/ctholocaust
Sun-Thu 1000-1700, Fri 1000-1300. Donation. Map 2, D7, p249

Cape Town's newest museum is also one of its best, comprising
an intelligent and shocking examination of the Holocaust. Exhibits
follow a historical route, starting with a look at anti-Semitism in
Europe in previous centuries, and then leading to the rise of
Nazism in Germany, the creation of ghettos, death camps and the
Final Solution, and liberation at the end of the war. Video footage,
photography, examples of Nazi propaganda and personal accounts
of the Holocaust produce a vividly haunting and shocking display.
The exhibits cleverly acknowledge South Africa's recent emergence
from apartheid and draw parallels between both injustices, as well
as looking at the link between South Africa's Greyshirts (who were
later assimilated into the National Party) and the Nazis. The local
context is highlighted further at the end of the exhibition, with
video accounts of Jews who survived the Holocaust and moved
to Cape Town.

National Gallery

Paddock Av, **T** 021-4651628, www.museums.org.za/sang *Mon
1300-1700, Tue-Sun 1000-1700. Donation. Map 2, D7, p249*

The National Gallery houses a permanent collection of local and
international art, as well as some interesting temporary exhibitions.
The original collection was bequeathed to the nation in 1871 by
Thomas Butterworth Bailey. Most of South Africa's best-known
artists are also represented, and the Hyman Liberman Hall is
devoted to exhibiting new South African art. Snacks and light
lunches are available at the *Gallery Café*.

Rust en Vreugd

78 Buitenkant St, **T** 021-4653628 , www.museums.org.za/rustv
reugd *Mon-Sat 0900-1600. Free with the Castle of Good Hope
ticket.* *Map 2, D8, p249*

A few hundred metres east of the National Gallery, hidden behind
a high whitewashed wall, is this 18th-century mansion. It was
declared a historical monument in 1940, and subsequently restored
to its best period. Today it houses six galleries displaying a unique
collection of watercolours, engravings and lithographs depicting
the history of the Cape. Commercial exhibitions are held in the
galleries upstairs.

South African Public Library

Queen Victoria St, **T** 021-4246320. *Mon-Fri 0900-1700. Map 2,
B7, p249*

Adjoining the gardens is the South African Public Library, behind
St George's Cathedral. Opened in 1818, it is the country's oldest
national reference library and was one of the first free libraries in
the world. Today it houses an excellent and important collection
of historic books covering South Africa. The building also has a
bookshop and an internet café.

Houses of Parliament

Government Av, **T** 021-4032460. *Map 2, B8, p249*

The Houses of Parliament was completed in 1885, and when the
Union was formed in 1910 it became the seat for the national parliament. In front of the building is a marble statue of Queen Victoria,
erected by public subscription in honour of her Golden Jubilee. It
was unveiled in 1890 by the then Governor, Sir Henry Loch. While
parliament is sitting, from January to June, it is possible to watch
from the visitors' gallery during the week. Overseas visitors must

PALM TREE MOSQUE

EST. 1807

Long Street

Long Street, home to the Palm Tree Mosque, is one of Cape Town's trendiest areas, lined with a jumble of street cafés, second-hand shops, restaurants and clubs.

show their passports and call in advance to watch debates. Guided tours of the chambers and Constitutional Assembly are also given.

St George's Cathedral
Corner of Government Av and Wale St. *Map 2, B8, p249*

The last building on Government Avenue is St George's Cathedral. The building you see today is comparatively new: it was built at the beginning of the 20th century, after the first church, based upon St Pancras Church in London, was turned down. The present cathedral was designed by Sir Herbert Baker. The cathedral has figured in the news a little more than one might expect, since up until June 1996 this was where Archbishop Desmond Tutu gave many of his famous sermons.

Slave Lodge
Corner of Adderley and Wale sts, **T** 021-4618280, www.museums. org.za/slavelodge *Mon-Sat 0930-1630. R5. Map 2, B8, p249*

Slave Lodge, previously known as the Cultural History Museum, is the second oldest building in Cape Town and has had a varied history, starting life as a lodge for slaves, and then becoming a library, a post office, the Cape Supreme Court, and finally a museum In 1966. Its most significant role, however, was as a slave lodge for the VOC (Dutch East India Company). Between 1679 and 1811 the building housed up to 1,000 slaves. Local indigenous groups were protected by the VOC from being enslaved; slaves were consequently imported from Madagascar, India, Indonesia and other parts of Africa, creating the most culturally varied slave society in the world.

Conditions at the lodge were terrible and up to 20% of the slaves died every year. Sadly only a glimpse of this history is displayed by the museum. Instead, much of the collection celebrates colonialism and includes rambling displays of British and VOC weapons, household goods, furniture and money, as well as relics from Japan and ancient Rome, Greece and Egypt. There is also a room on the 'Cape Kaleidoscope', representing the history of Cape Town, and a display explaining some of the history of slavery. Perhaps the most interesting feature of the museum is a series of plaques describing the function of each room within the slave lodge. The museum's planners are now in the process of restructuring much of the museum – many of the colonial collections will be replaced with displays depicting slavery in the Cape and the lasting effects it has had on South African society.

Groote Kerk
Corner of Adderley and Spin sts. *1030-1200, 1400-1500, weekdays. Free guided tours.* Map 2, B8, p249

Nearby is one of Cape Town's older corners, Church Square, site of the Groote Kerk. Up until 1834 the square was used as a venue for the **auctioning of slaves** from the Slave Lodge, which faced onto the square. All transactions took place under a tree – a concrete plaque marks the old tree's position.

The Groote Kerk was the first church of the **Dutch Reformed** faith to be built in South Africa – building started in 1678 and it was consecrated in 1704. The present church, built between 1836 and 1841, is a somewhat dull grey building designed and built by Hermann Schutte after a fire had destroyed most of the original building. Many of the old gravestones were built into the base of the church walls, the most elaborate of which is the tombstone of Baron van Rheede van Oudtshoorn. Two of the Cape's early governors are buried here – Simon van der Stel (1679-99), and Ryk Tulbagh (1751-71). Of particular note is the beautiful pulpit carved by Anton Anreith, whose work can also be seen at Groot Constantia. The two baroque heraldic lions which support the pulpit are said to represent the power of faith.

● *Look out for the special pews with their own locked doors. These belonged to wealthy families who didn't want to pray with commoners.*

South Africa is the only place
in the world where a revolution
has been made to the accompaniment
of four-part harmonies

Abdullah Ibrahim
The pianist, popularly known as Dollar Brand,
arguably the godfather of Cape Jazz

City Hall and Grand Parade

Darling St. *Visitors can get a Holiday Visitors' Card valid for 3 months for a small fee. Map 2, B9, p249*

From Adderley Street, a short walk down Darling Street takes you to the City Hall and the Grand Parade. The latter is the largest open space in Cape Town and was originally used for garrison parades before the Castle was completed. Today the oak-lined parade is used as a car park and twice a week it is taken over by a busy market. After his release from prison, **Nelson Mandela** made his first speech to over 100,000 people on the Grand Parade from the City Hall on 9 May 1994. The neo-classical City Hall, built to celebrate Queen Victoria's Golden Jubilee, overlooks the parade. The hall is now headquarters of the Cape Town Symphony Orchestra and houses the City Library. The library reading room has local, national and international newspapers.

Castle of Good Hope

Darling St, www.castleofgoodhope.co.za *0900-1600. R15, includes a guided tour and entry to Rust en Vreugd. Entry from the Grand Parade side. Map 2, B10/11, p249*

Beyond the Grand Parade is the main entrance of South Africa's oldest colonial building, the Castle of Good Hope. Work started in 1666 by Commander Zacharias Wagenaer and was completed in 1679. Its original purpose was for the Dutch East India Company to defend the Cape from rival European powers, and today it is an imposing sight, albeit a rather gloomy one. Under the British, the Castle served as government headquarters and since 1917 it has been the headquarters of the South African Defence Force.

Today the castle is home to three museums. The **William Fehr Collection** is one of South Africa's finest displays of furnishings, reflecting the social and political history of the Cape. There are landscapes by John Thomas Baines and William Huggins,

17th-century Japanese porcelain and 18th-century Indonesian furniture. Upstairs is an absurdly huge dining table which seats 104, in a room still used for state dinners.

To the left of the Fehr Collection is the **Secunde's House**. The Secunde was second in charge of the settlement at the Cape, responsible for administrative duties for the Dutch East India Company. None of the three rooms contain original furniture from the Castle, but they do recreate the conditions under which an official for the Dutch East India Company would have lived in the 17th, 18th and early 19th centuries.

The third museum is the **Military Museum**, a rather indifferent collection depicting the conflicts of early settlers. More absorbing are the regimental displays of uniforms and medals. Expect to have any bags checked since the castle is still used as the regional offices for the National Defence Force. There are free guided tours at 1100, 1200 and 1400. These are informative and fun, although a little short. Tour highlights include the torture chambers, cells, views from the battlements and Dolphin Court, where Lady Anne Barnard was supposedly seen bathing in the nude by the sentries. While waiting for a tour you can enjoy coffee and cakes at a small café, or explore van der Stel's restored wine cellars, where you can taste and buy wines. Audio tapes can also be hired and provide a 45-minute tour. There is full ceremonial Changing of the Guard at noon.

★ District Six Museum

25a Buitenkant St, **T** 021-4618745, www.districtsix.co.za *Mon-Sat 0900-1600. Map 2, C9, p 249*

Housed in the Methodist Church, this museum is one of Cape Town's most powerful exhibitions and gives a fascinating glimpse of the stupidity and horror of apartheid. District Six was once the vibrant, cosmopolitan heart of Cape Town, a largely coloured inner city suburb renowned for its jazz scene. In February 1966, PW Botha, then Minister of Community Development, formally

★ Karnaval

Cape Town's biggest and most raucous carnival is when the city's ethnic community celebrates the advent of the New Year. Karnaval, held to pay tribute to the tradition of the minstrel entertainers who stopped by Cape Town on American ocean liners over a hundred years ago, involves numerous festivals, competitions and extravagant parades. It is quite the spectacle.

proclaimed District Six a "white" group area. Over the next 15 years, an estimated 60,000 people were given notice to give up their homes and moved to the new townships on the Cape Flats. The area was razed, and to this day remains largely undeveloped.

The museum contains a collection of photographs, articles and personal accounts depicting life before and after the removals. Highlights include a large map covering most of the ground floor, upon which ex-residents have been encouraged to mark their homes and local sights. The "Namecloth" is particularly poignant: a 1.5m-wide length of cloth has been provided for ex-residents to write down their comments, part of which hangs by the entrance. It has grown to over 1 km in the last eight years, and features some moving and insightful thoughts.

Adderley Street and Heerengracht
Map 2, B8/A9, p249

Adderley Street is one of the city's busiest shopping areas, and is sadly marred by a number of 1960s and 70s eyesores, but it does still boast some impressive bank buildings. On the corner of Darling Street is the **Standard Bank Building** (1880), a grand structure built shortly after the diamond wealth from Kimberley began to reach Cape Town. The exterior has a central dome surmounted by the figure Britannia, but it is the main banking hall which is of most interest, with all the original Victorian features remaining largely intact. Diagonally across Adderley Street is the equally impressive **Barclays Bank Building** (1933), a fine Ceres sandstone building which was the last major work by Sir Herbert Baker in South Africa. Though built 50 years after the Standard Bank, its interior is just as detailed in design.

! Cape Town is booming as a film location on account of the
• settings, perfect light and low costs. Adderley Street is often
used to depict modern shopping streets in US cities.

At the corner of Adderley Street and Strand Street stands a modern shopping mall complex, the **Sanlam Golden Acre**. On the lower level of the complex the remains of an aqueduct and a reservoir dating from 1663 can be viewed. The line of black floor tiles close to the escalator which links the centre with the railway station mark the position of the original shoreline before any reclamation work began in Table Bay. Continuing down towards the docks, Adderley Street passes Cape Town Railway Station. At the junction with Hans Strijdom Street is a large roundabout with a central fountain and a bronze statue of **Jan van Riebeeck**, given to the city by Cecil Rhodes in 1899. Reibeeck was the first European to settle at the Cape, arriving in 1652 with 90 others. At the bottom end of Adderley Street are statues of Bartholomew Dias, a Portuguese explorer who was the first European to reach the Cape of Good Hope in 1487, and Maria van Riebeeck, wife of Jan van Riebeeck, donated respectively by the Portuguese and Dutch governments in 1952 for Cape Town's tercentenary celebrations.

In front of the Medical Centre on Heerengracht is the **Scott Memorial**. What is on show is in fact a bronze replica; the original, a stone argosy, was smashed by vandals. Its location has barely changed, but when it was unveiled in 1916 it was on the approach to a pier at the foot of Adderley Street, a further indication of how much additional land has been reclaimed from Table Bay over the years. The palm trees once graced a marine promenade in this area. Up until the 1850s there was a canal running the full length of Heerengracht and Adderley streets. This was covered over as the city prospered and traffic congestion became a problem.

Koopmans-De Wet House

Strand St, **T** 021-4242473, www.museums.org.za/koopmans
Tue-Sat 0930-1630. Small fee. Map 2, A8, p249

Just off St George's Mall, on a pedestrian road lined with shops and cafés, is the delightfully peaceful Koopmans-De Wet House.

Surviving in the midst of ugly modern buildings and the bustle of central Cape Town, it is one of the more interesting museums in town. The house is named in memory of Marie Koopmans-De Wet, a prominent figure in cultured Cape Society, who lived here between 1834 and 1906. The inside has been restored to reflect the period of her grandparents who lived here in the late 18th century. Though not too cluttered there is a fascinating collection of furnishings which gives the house an appealing, tranquil feel. The back of the house has a shaded courtyard and the original stables with the slave quarters above.

Greenmarket Square
Map 2, A8, p249 See also Shopping, p190

This is the old heart of Cape Town and the second oldest square in the city. It has long been a meeting place, and during the 19th century it became a vegetable market. In 1834 it took on the significant role of being the site where the declaration of freeing all slaves was made. Today it remains a popular meeting place and is lined with outdoor cafés and restaurants. A busy daily market sprawls across the cobbles, with stalls selling African crafts, jewellery and clothes.

Most of the buildings around the square reflect the city's history. Dominating one side is a *Holiday Inn*, housed in what was once the headquarters of the Shell Oil Company – note the shell motifs on its exterior. Diagonally opposite is the **Old Town House** (1751), originally built to house the town guard. It became the first town hall in 1840 when Cape Town became a municipality. Much of the exterior remains unchanged, and with its decorative plaster mouldings and fine curved fanlights is one of the best preserved Cape Baroque exteriors in the city. Today the white double-storeyed building houses the **Michaelis collection** of Flemish and Dutch paintings. Next to the *Tudor Hotel* is the second oldest building in the square – the **Metropolitan Methodist Church** (1876). This

Rose Corner Café

The Bo-Kaap, Cape Town's historic Islamic quarter, is famous for its rows of pastel painted houses, busy mosques, spice shops and curry houses.

is the only high Victorian church in Cape Town and has a tall spire with a unique series of miniature grotesques decorating its exterior.

● *If you're interested in antiques, walk out of the square past the Methodist church to Church Street. The area between Burg and Long Streets is the venue for a daily antique street market.*

Long Street
Map 2, B6-A8, p248-249 See also Bars and clubs, p165

This stretch is one of the trendiest in Cape Town, and gets particularly lively at night. Lined with street cafés, fashionable shops, bars, clubs and backpacker lodges, it has a distinctly young feel about it, but is also home to some fine old city buildings. One of Cape Town's late Victorian gems is at number 117, now an antique shop. On the outside is an unusual cylindrical turret with curved windows; inside is a fine cast iron spiral staircase leading to a balustraded gallery.

South African Missionary House Museum, or Sendinggestig Museum, at number 40, is one of the more interesting buildings on Long Street. It is the oldest mission church in South Africa, built between 1802-04 as the mother church for missionary work carried out in rural areas. Though utilized by directors and members of the South African Missionary Society, it was more commonly used for religious and literacy instruction of slaves in Cape Town. By 1960 most of its congregation had been moved to the Cape Flats or died. Inside, there is a permanent display of missionary work throughout the Cape, and behind the pulpit are display cabinets showing early cash accounts and receipts for transactions such as the transfer of slaves.

★ The Bo-Kaap
Map 2, p248

A few blocks west along Wale Street is the Bo-Kaap, Cape Town's
historical Islamic quarter and one of the city's most interesting

residential areas. Its streets are characterized by brightly-painted Georgian facades, tightly packed along cobbled streets. Although fast becoming popular with a yuppie class, the area has managed to retain much of its ambience and strong identity. Bo-Kaap residents are descendants of slaves imported by the Dutch in the 17th century – although they are still referred to as Cape Malays, only a tiny percentage originated in Malaysia. Most came from India, Madagascar and West Africa. **Bo-Kaap Museum**, housed in an attractive 18th-century house, is dedicated to the community and contains the furnishings of a wealthy 19th-century Muslim family. In the front room there is one item of original furniture, a table inlaid with mother of pearl. In the prayer room, *langgar*, is an old Koran and *tasbeh* beads set in front of the mihrab alcove, while the courtyard holds a collection of coaches and early carts. Unfortunately none of the items have any explanatory labels. The house itself is one of the oldest buildings in Cape Town surviving in its original form. It was built by Jan de Waal for artisans in 1763. It was here that Abu Bakr Effendi started the first Arabic school and wrote some important articles on Islamic Law. He originally came to Cape Town as a guest of the British Government to try and settle religious differences amongst the Cape Muslims.

Victoria and Alfred Waterfront

Cape Town's original Victorian harbour is the city's most popular attraction. The whole area was completely restored in the early 1990s, and today it is a lively district packed with restaurants, bars and shops. Original buildings stand shoulder to shoulder with mock-Victorian shopping centres, museums and al fresco restaurants, all crowding along a waterside walkway with Table Mountain looming in the background. Until very recently, the Waterfront was seen as something of a hedonistic playground for tourists – the only reason for coming here was to shop and eat, and many argued that the area was over-sanitized and artificial. While it certainly remains touristy, recent developments have changed its image somewhat. *The opening of the* **Nelson Mandela Gateway** *to nearby Robben Island, with a brand new museum depicting prison life, has gone some way in raising the area's profile. It is also becoming known as an* **outdoor music venue**, *hosting live acts during the annual Jazz Festival. And despite being geared towards tourists it remains a* **working harbour**, *which provides much of the area's real charm.*

▶▶ *See Sleeping p118, Eating and drinking p141, Shopping p189*

Sights

Clock Tower
Map 3, C11, p251

A number of original buildings remain around the basins and are an interesting diversion from the razzmatazz of the shops and restaurants. At the narrow entrance to the Alfred Basin, on the Berties Landing side, is the original Clock Tower, built in 1882 to house the Port Captain's office. This is in the form of a red octagonal Gothic- style tower and stands just in front of the Clock Tower Centre, the newest collection of shops, offices and restaurants on the Waterfront. The ground floor of the Clock Tower houses an information kiosk and the original tide gauge mechanism which enabled the exact depths in the basin to be checked. Sadly the other rooms are now closed to the public, although it is sometimes possible to climb to the roof, allowing fine views of the surrounds. The Clock Tower Centre, opposite,

---

! The area derives its name from the two harbour basins around which it developed. Construction began in 1860, when Prince Alfred, Queen Victoria's second son, tipped the first load of stone to start the building. Alfred Basin could not handle the increased shipping so Victoria basin was built.

houses the new Nelson Mandela Gateway to Robben Island, from where you catch the main ferry to the island. A museum has now been opened depicting prison life.

Union Castle Building

T 021-4195957. *Tue-Sun 0900-1800. R10. Map 3, C10, p251 See also Kids, p215*

Walking across the swing bridge from the Clock Tower (look out for the frolicking Cape Fur seals as you cross), you come to the *Victoria and Alfred Hotel*. Opposite here is a stocky square building known as Union Castle Building (1919), designed by the firm of architects owned by Sir Herbert Baker. The Union Steamship Company and the Castle Line both ran monthly mail ships between Britain and South Africa, in the late 19th century. In 1900 they amalgamated and from then on mail was delivered every week. The last Union Castle ship to sail to England with the mail was the Windsor Castle in 1977. The building now houses **Telekom Exploratorium**, a small museum focusing on technology and communication, aimed at children.

Victoria and Alfred Hotel

Dock Rd. *Map 3, C10, p251*

Behind the Union Castle Building is this luxury four-star hotel. It was originally built as a coal store before being converted into Union Castle's warehouse and customs baggage store. It had a third floor but this was destroyed in a fire in 1939. This building is a perfect example of how effective restoration can be, and how with a bit of imagination a whole area can be given a new lease of life. This was the first hotel to be opened at the Waterfront and it is an important part of the success of the whole venture.

Time Ball Tower
Dock Rd. *Map 3, C10, p251*

On the other side of the road above the car park, is the Time Ball Tower. This dates from 1894; its purpose was to act as an accurate reference for ships' navigators to set their clocks as the ball on the roof fell. Correct time was vital for the navigator to be able to determine precise longitude before the development of more modern equipment. Beside the tower is a 100-year-old **Dragon Tree** from the Canary Islands, and next to the tree is the original **Harbour Master's Residence**, 1860.

Two Oceans Aquarium
Dock Rd, **T** 021-4183823, www.aquarium.co.za *0930-1800. Daily feeds at 1530. R45. Map 3, C9, p251 See also Kids, p215*

The top attraction on the Waterfront is this aquarium, focusing on the unique Cape marine environment created by the meeting of the Atlantic and Indian Oceans. The display begins with a walk through the Indian Ocean, where visitors follow a route past tanks filled with a multitude of colourful fish, turtles, seahorses and octopuses. Highlights here include giant spider crabs and phosphorescent jellyfish, floating in a mesmerising circular current. From here you walk past touch pools, where children can pick up spiky starfish and slimy sea slugs. The basement holds the Alpha Activity Centre, where free puppet shows and face painting keep children busy. The main wall here is part of the Diving Animals pool, where you can watch Cape fur seals dart and dive before the glass. On the first floor is the Story of Water exhibit, an interesting enough display although the resident African penguins seem rather confined in their enclosure. Next is the Kelp Forest, an extraordinary tangle of giant kelp which sways drunkenly in the artificial tides. The highlight is the predators exhibit, an enormous tank complete with glass tunnel, holding ragged-tooth sharks, eagle rays, turtles, and some impressively large hunting fish. There are daily feeds at 1530. It is also possible to dive in the predator's tank. Certified divers can pay R350 to dive for half an hour; book a day in advance. It is a very safe but hair-raising experience, and thoroughly recommended for a first-time shark dive.

★ Robben Island

Tours are run by the Robben Island Museum, **T** 021-4191300, www.robben-island.org.za *0900-1800. R100 for adults, R50 for children under 17. Book a day ahead as tickets sell out. Boats leave on the hour between 0900 and 1500. Allow 3 hours. Map, inside back cover*

Lying 13 km off Green Point's shores, Robben Island is best known as the notorious prison that held many of the ANC's most prominent members, including **Nelson Mandela** and **Walter Sisulu**. It was originally named by the Dutch, after the term for seals, *'rob'* – actually a misnomer as none are found here. The island's history of occupation started in 1806, when John Murray was granted permission by the British to conduct whaling from the island. During this period the authorities started to use the island as a dumping ground for common convicts; these were brought back to the mainland in 1843, and their accommodation was deemed suitable for lepers and the mentally ill. These were in turn moved to the mainland between 1913 and 1931, and the island entered a new era as a military base during the Second World War. In 1960 the military passed control of the island over to the Department of Prisons, and it remained a prison until 1996. On 1 December 1999 the island was declared a World Heritage Site by UNESCO.

Robben Island's effectiveness as a prison did not rest simply with the fact that escape was virtually impossible. The authorities

! All tour guides on Robben Island were once political prisoners
● here, offering an honest insight to prison life under apartheid.

anticipated that the idea of "out of sight, out of mind" would be particularly applicable here, and to a certain extent they were correct. Certainly, its isolation did much to break the spirit of political prisoners, not least **Robert Sobukwe**'s. Sobukwe was the leader of the Pan African Congress, and was kept in solitary confinement for nine years. Other political prisoners were spared that at least, although in 1971 they were separated from common law prisoners, as they were deemed a 'bad' influence. Conditions were harsh, with forced hard labour and routine beatings. Much of the daily running of the maximum security prison was designed to reinforce racial divisions: all the warders, and none of the prisoners, were white; black prisoners, unlike those deemed coloured, had to wear short trousers and were given smaller food rations. Contact with the outside world was virtually non-existent – visitors had to apply for permission six months in advance and were allowed to stay for just half an hour. Newspapers were banned and letters were limited to one every six months. Yet despite these measures, the B-Section, which housed Mandela and other major political prisoners, became the international focus of the fight against apartheid.

A protective ring

Karamats are the tombs of Imams who lived and worked with the Muslim community of Cape Town. They are dotted around Cape Town in a circle that is believed to provide the city with a protective spiritual boundary, preventing natural disasters. Surprisingly little is made of the Karamats in tourist literature, but for devout Cape Muslims they are very important. Before embarking upon *haj* a local muslim will visit each Karamat in turn. There is one here, on Robben Island. Others can be seen on the slopes of Signal Hill and in Constantia Valley.

The last political prisoners left the island in 1991.

Tours begin with a drive around the key sites on the island, including Sobukwe's house, the lime quarry where Mandela was forced to work, the leper cemetery, and the houses of former warders. It is also possible to view wildlife – as a prison, the area was strictly protected, allowing the fish and bird populations to flourish. There are over 100 species of bird on the island, and it is an important breeding site for African penguins.

Atlantic Seaboard

*Stretching from Green Point to the Cape of Good Hope, this is the peninsula's most spectacular coastline, at times clinging dramatically to the **Twelve Apostles**, the spine of mountains stretching south. The area is best known for its beautiful beaches, including famous Clifton, the spot to mingle with the bronzed glitterati, from Cape Town socialites to supermodels.*

*Closest to the city are the rather less glamorous suburbs of **Green Point** and **Sea Point**, both lacking beaches and crammed with modern apartment blocks, but each with a different appeal. Green Point is nightlife central and the main gay and lesbian hub, while Sea Point has more of a family seaside holiday feel. Further along are **Clifton** and **Camps Bay**, the latter offering a perfect arch of palm-fringed sand backed with seafood restaurants. From here the rocky coast is surprisingly undeveloped, with just a handful of holiday homes backing onto surfing beaches, before the coastal road passes through **Hout Bay** with its beautiful rock promontories and working harbour, dishing up fresh fish and chips. The bay marks the beginning of **Chapman's Peak Drive**, perhaps the most spectacular stretch of road in South Africa, although only part of it is open to drivers.*

▸▸ *See Sleeping p119, Eating and drinking p143, Bars and clubs p169, Gay and lesbian p207*

◉ Sights

Green Point and Sea Point
Map 3, p250 and Map 4, p252

Although the closest seaside areas to the city, they lack much of the charm and character found in the rest of Cape Town. Both are a mixture of high-rise apartment blocks lining the rocky seafront, and more attractive Victorian bungalows creeping up the slopes of Signal Hill. Green Point has become the focus of Cape Town's gay scene, with a great selection of fashionable daytime cafés and late-night clubs. Sea Point has an excellent selection of accommodation, as well as a good range of shops and restaurants more geared towards families. The beach is unsafe for swimming, although there are a couple of rock pools, including Graaf's Pool (men only) and Milton's Pool.

★ Clifton Beach
Map 1, B2, p246

Cape Town's best-known beaches stretch along Clifton, and are renowned as the playground of the young and wealthy – this is the place to see and be seen. Other than being hotpots of high society, Clifton's four sheltered beaches are stunning, small arches of powder-soft white sand sloping gently into turquoise water. The beaches are divided by rocky outcrops and are numbered: First, Second, Third and Fourth. Each has a distinct character – if you're bronzed and beautiful, head to First beach. More demure visitors will feel comfortable on Fourth, which is popular with families,

!
Clifton and Camps Bay have the most sought-after real estate in Africa. Serious celebrities – Michael Jackson and Will Smith included – were reportedly looking for houses here.

while Third is the main gay beach, although again perfect pecs are essential. The sunbathing and surfing are good on all the beaches, but the water is cold. Most of the relatively small-scale development has been behind the beaches against the cliff face (some impressive houses can be glimpsed through the greenery). Be warned that there is limited parking and it's a steep climb down footpaths to the beach.

Camps Bay
Map 5, p253

Following the coast south, you soon skirt around a hill and come out over Camps Bay, a long arch of sand backed by the Twelve Apostles. This is one of the most beautiful (and most photographed) beaches in the world, but the calm cobalt water belies its chilliness. The sand is also less sheltered than at Clifton, and sunbathing here on a windy day can be quite painful. But there are other distractions; the beachfront is lined with a number of excellent seafood restaurants, and having a sundowner followed by a superb meal is the perfect ending to a day in Cape Town.

The drive between Camps Bay and Hout Bay runs along the slopes of the Twelve Apostles and is stunning. Apart from the turning to **Llandudno**, there is no easy access to the coast until you reach Hout Bay. Llandudno itself is a small, exclusive settlement with a fine beach and excellent surf.

Hout Bay
Map 1, E1, p246

Hout Bay may seem strangely familiar – little surprise considering how often it is featured on postcards and coffee table books. It is a perfect cove with a white sandy beach, clear blue waters and a busy fishing harbour. From here the famous Chapman's Peak Drive begins, and as the sun sets in the summer months every pullover

★ **Best**

Beaches

along the road gets occupied by groups watching the sun go down with a drink in hand.

Unless you're planning on taking a boat trip from the harbour, the best place to leave your car is in the car park opposite *Chapman's Peak Hotel*. From here you can easily walk to all the shops or down to the beach.

Before Cape Town had established itself as the foremost port in the district, Hout Bay was an important natural sheltered anchorage. Today, activity centres around two locations: at the western end of the bay is the fishing harbour; at the other end is a collection of shops and popular restaurants. By the harbour is a commercial complex known as **Mariners Wharf**, the first of its kind in South Africa and a very popular attraction. It is based upon Fisherman's Wharf in San Francisco, and a lot of thought has gone into the building. The restaurant serves a wide selection of fresh seafood and has a wine list to match. Another attraction is **Snoekies Fresh Fish Market**, close to the harbour gates. Even if you're not intending to buy anything it is well worth the visit to see the huge variety of fish that are caught off this coast.

Drumbeat Charters conduct tours to see seals on **Duiker Island** in season (August to April). Trips depart at 1130, 1330 and 1530, cost R35 and take about an hour. It's a good opportunity to admire the Cape peninsula from the sea.

World of Birds, at Valley Road, is set in 4 km of open land in walk-through aviaries, with over 400 species of birds. A popular attraction, but perhaps a little strange for an overseas visitor who has seen the birds when strolling in the mountains or at Zandvlei. The fact remains you can see hundreds of birds in South Africa without having to look too hard.

★ Chapman's Peak Drive
Map 1, E2, p246

It is worth hiring a car for a day just to drive along Chapman's Peak Drive, a breathtaking 15-km route carved into the cliffs 600 m above the sea. The views of the coast and ocean are outstanding and one of the Cape's highlights. The best time to drive along here is close to sunset in the summer, but the views of Hout Bay are recommended at any time. The original road was built between 1915 and 1922. After a series of major rock falls in early 2000 much of the road remains closed. It is due to re-open by the end of 2002, though this seems unlikely. Check before you go. It is still possible to drive up to the highest viewpoints from the Hout Bay side.

Noordhoek
Map 1, F2, p246

The greatest attraction here is the 8-km long deserted beach with a couple of tidal lagoons behind it which offer excellent bird watching. The Chapman's Peak Trading Centre on Beach Road is a good shopping spot, including a Kakapo farm stall and bakery, Milkwood Craft Co-op, curios and clothes. This is also a popular setting for horse riding along the shore.

Kommetjie
Map 1, G1, p247

Driving along the Atlantic side of the peninsula, you could miss Kommetjie altogether if you were to follow the signs for Ocean View. Kommetjie means 'little basin', a reference to the natural inlet in the rocks which has been developed into a tidal pool. The settlement is small with a pub, restaurant, caravan park and little else. It is, however, a major surfing spot and Long Beach to the north is always busy with surfers, even in winter. There is also an interesting walk along Long Beach to the wreck of the *Kakapo*, offering a rare opportunity to examine a wreck at close quarters without having to don full scuba equipment. The *Kakapo* is a steamship which was beached here in May 1900 on her maiden voyage when the captain apparently mistook Chapman's Peak for Cape Point during a storm.

★ Cape of Good Hope Nature Reserve
T 021-7018692, www.cpnp.co.za   *0600-1800 Oct-Mar, 0700-1700 Apr-Sep. R25. Visiting in your own vehicle is recommended (65 km from the centre). Several companies do organize good day trips however.   Map 1, K3, p247   See also Boat tours, p25*

The Cape of Good Hope Nature Reserve is one of Cape Town's highlights, a strikingly wild region straddling the ground between the Atlantic Seaboard and False Bay. The reserve was established in 1939 to protect the unique flora and fauna of this stretch of coast. It is an integral part of the Cape Floristic Kingdom, the smallest but richest of the world's six floral kingdoms. A frequently quoted statistic is that within the 7,750 ha of the reserve there are as many different plant species as there are in the whole of the British Isles. In addition to this there are several different species of antelope: eland, bontebok, springbok, Cape grysbok, red hartebeest and grey rhebok, as well as the elusive Cape mountain zebra, snakes, tortoises and pesky baboons. Needless to say, it's a popular place to visit. If possible avoid going at the weekend or during school holidays.

Although the strong winds and the low lying vegetation are not ideal for birds, over 250 species have been recorded here, of which about 100 are known to breed within the reserve. There are plenty of vantage points where you can watch open-sea birds – you should expect to see the Cape gannet, shy albatross, sooty shearwater, Sabine's gull and Cory's shearwater. In the Strandveld vegetation along the coast you can expect to see many fruit eating birds such as the Cape robin and bully canary. Around Sirkels Vlei you will find some freshwater birds. Finally there are a couple of rarities: the white-rumped sandpiper from South America, macaroni penguins from Antarctica, and the purple gallinule from the US have all been seen within the reserve. The Veld Museum issues a check list of 100 birds. Alongside each name is a code telling you the typical habitat and the bird's resident status.

Cape Point Lighthouse is nothing special in itself, adorned with a fair amount of graffiti, but the climb up here is well worth it for the best view of Cape Point. You can take the funicular to the top, but the 20-minute walk allows better views of the coast. If you are reasonably fit and have a good head for heights, there is a spectacular walk to the modern lighthouse at Diaz Point. From the renovated old lighthouse you can see the path running along the left side of the narrow cliff that makes up the point. The round trip takes about 30 minutes. Do not attempt it if it is windy – the winds around the Cape can reach up to 55 knots (100 km per hour). As you look down from the lighthouse at Cape Point it is easy to see how ships could suffer on a dark night in a storm, especially before the lighthouse was built. There are 23 wrecks in the waters around the Cape, but only five can be seen when walking in the reserve: *Thomas T Tucker*, 1942; *Nolloth*, 1964; *Phyllisia*, 1968; *Shir Yib*, 1970 (at Diaz Beach) and *The Tania*, 1972, the most recent wreck which can be seen at Buffels Bay. The first wreck was the *Flying Dutchman*

Cape of Good Hope Nature Reserve
Just a short drive from the city centre is this wild and rugged area, with its empty beaches, wildlife and breathtaking views.

in 1680, which has since become famous as a ghost ship. The most famous sighting was by midshipman King George V in 1881.

● *There are several marked paths and maps are available from the Veld Museum. One of the most spectacular walks is along the coast from Rooikrans towards Buffels Bay. Look out for the wreck,* The Tania, *1972.*

Southern Suburbs

*Hugging the lower slopes of Table Mountain and stretching southeast away from the city centre, towards Constantia and False Bay, are Cape Town's Southern Suburbs. These encompass the bulk of Cape Town's suburban sprawl, once the enclave of largely affluent whites but today an interesting mix of areas with a number of attractions. The suburbs start with **Woodstock** just outside the City Bowl on the slopes of **Devil's Peak**, a mostly working-class coloured area which is fast becoming yuppified. They continue all the way around the mountain, finishing just before **False Bay** in the beautiful wine-growing area of **Constantia** with its manicured gardens, forests and fortified mansions. Rolling away from the mountain's slopes are the **Cape Flats**, a vast sprawl of coloured and black townships and mushrooming shanty towns, home to the majority of Cape Town's residents yet rarely visited by tourists. The main draw in the Southern Suburbs are the magnificent **Kirstenbosch Botanical Gardens** and Constantia's historical vineyards and elegant hotels, but there are a number of more unconventional attractions – like bar-hopping in **Observatory**, watching a rugby match at **Newlands** or shopping in some of Cape Town's glitziest malls.*

▸▸ *See Sleeping p123, Eating and drinking p148, Bars and clubs p171*

Although a car is the best way to visit, it is possible to reach all by train – the Metro service between the city centre and Simon's Town runs through all the suburbs. Keep in mind that it's best to avoid the trains when it's not busy.

◉ Sights

Woodstock and Observatory
Map 6 and 7, p253 and 254

The first suburb, **Woodstock**, is a mixed commercial and residential area, historically a working-class coloured district. In the 19th century it was a thriving community, when it was known as Papendorp. It became a municipality in 1881 and the local residents were invited to choose a new name. The most popular drinking haunt at the time was the *Woodstock Hotel*, and so the suburb got its present name. Today it seems run down and a little depressing, although the back streets are an attractive mesh of beautiful Victorian bungalows, many of which are being snapped up by a new influx of young professionals.

Observatory is an attractive area of tightly packed houses, narrow streets and student hangouts. In recent years, it has managed to create its own special ambience, and once settled here you can quickly forget about the town centre or Waterfront. Being close to the university, there is a wide range of trendy bars, cafés and restaurants catering for a mixed scene of students, bohemian types and budget backpackers. This is a good area to stay in and has an enjoyably liberal atmosphere not so easily found in some of the other suburbs. The observatory after which the suburb is named is where Station Road intersects Liesbeeck Parkway. Aside from making astronomical observations the observatory was responsible for accurate standard time in South Africa. It has also been an important meteorological centre and has a seismograph which records earthquakes around the world. Observatory is also where you'll

> **!** Mark Shuttleworth, Africa's first man in space – or Afronaut – is originally from Cape Town and studied at UCT (University of Cape Town) before making his millions.

find the Groot Schuur Hospital on Main Road, the site of the world's first heart transplant.

Mowbray, Rosebank and Rondebosch
Map 1, C4, p246

The next suburbs of Mowbray, Rosebank and Rondebosch lie just below the University of Cape Town. Again, they are popular with students and have a good selection of restaurants and shops. Early written accounts describe the area as wild country, with the farmers frequently losing livestock to hyenas, lion and leopards – an image that is hard to imagine as you sit in the evening rush hour traffic jam on Rhodes Drive. In Rondebosch is Groot Schuur, the Prime Minister's official residence and Westbrooke, home of the State President.

A lesser-known but fascinating tourist attraction in the area is the **Irma Stern Museum** (*Tue-Sat 1000-1700. R8*). Irma Stern was one of South Africa's pioneering artists and her lovely house, on Cecil Road, displays a mixture of her own works, a collection of artefacts from across Africa, and some fine pieces of antique furniture from overseas – 17th-century Spanish chairs, 19th-century German oak furniture and Swiss *mardi gras* masks. Her portraits are particularly poignant and those of her close friends are superb, while her religious art is rather more disturbing. Stern's studio, complete with paint brushes and palettes, has been left as it was when she died. The most important African items were collected in the Congo and Zanzibar. Of particular note is the Buli Stool, one of only 20 known carvings by a master carver from southeast Zaire.

The best-known attraction in the area is the **Rhodes Memorial**, off Rhodes Drive, by the Rondebosch turning. The imposing granite memorial to Cecil John Rhodes (Cape Prime Minister from 1890-96) was designed by Francis Masey and Sir Herbert Baker. Four bronze lions flank a wide flight of steps which lead up to a

Greek temple. The temple houses an immense bronze head of Rhodes, wrought by JM Swan. Above the head are the words "slave to the spirit and life work of Cecil John Rhodes who loved and served South Africa". At the base of the steps is an immense bronze mounted figure of Physical Energy given to South Africa by GF Watts, a well regarded sculptor of the time; the original stands in Hyde Park, London. Other than the memorial, the great attraction here is the magnificent view of the Cape Flats and the Southern Suburbs. Behind the memorial are a number of popular trails leading up the slopes of Devil's Peak.

● *Tucked away here is an excellent little tea house set in a garden of blue hydrangeas which serves good cheesecake, sandwiches and cream teas – a popular spot, especially for lunch at weekends.*

South of Rondebosch
Map 1, C4/D4, p246

By this point the Southern Suburbs have reached right around Devil's Peak and the shadowy peaks now dominating the views represent an unfamiliar view of Table Mountain. **Newlands** backs right up to the slopes of the mountain and is probably best known for being the home to Western Province Rugby Union and the beautiful Newlands cricket test ground. Sports fans shouldn't miss the chance of seeing a game here. There are several good hotels and guesthouses in the area. Also in Newlands is the **Rugby Museum**, on Boundary Road, housed in the Sports Medical Research Institute Building. The collection commemorates the history of the sport in the country and is also home to the Currie Cup, the premier domestic competition trophy.

Claremont offers little of interest. On the main road is the upmarket Cavendish Square Complex, another of South Africa's shopping malls. Nearby however, are **Ardene Gardens**, a Victorian park which has escaped the developer. These were first planted in 1845 by Ralph Arderne, who was so charmed by the

Cape while en route for Australia that he decided to settle here instead. He succeeded in creating a garden that would represent the flora of the world. Today the arboretum with specimens from all over the world is probably the best collection of trees in South Africa. The gardens were declared a historical monument in 1962.

A little further along the main road takes you to **Wynberg**. Apart from a few curio shops, the main attraction here is the district known as **Little Chelsea**. This is a group of well-preserved 19th-century homes which have infinitely more character than most new buildings in Cape Town.

★ Kirstenbosch Botanical Gardens

T 021-7998783, weekends **T** 021-7998620, www.nbi.ac.za *Sep-Mar 0800-1900, Apr-Aug 0800-1800. R15. By far the easiest way of getting here is by car. Otherwise there are trains to the nearest station at Mowbray. From here, there is an erratic bus service or a long walk. Alternatively, take a Rikki – they will pick up and drop off at any time other than rush hour. Map 1, D3, p246*

Kirstenbosch are South Africa's oldest, largest and most exquisite botanical gardens. They are among the finest in the world, their setting alone is incomparable. The gardens stretch up the eastern slopes of Table Mountain, merging seamlessly with the *fynbos* (area of low shrubs) of the steep slopes above. Cecil Rhodes bought Kirstenbosch farm in 1895 and promptly presented the site to the people of South Africa with the intention that it become a botanical garden. It was not until 1913 that Kirstenbosch was proclaimed a National Botanical Garden – the Anglo-Boer War had caused the delay.

As with all botanical gardens they are divided into smaller specialist gardens. The Fragrance garden, the Dell, the Medicinal Plants garden and Van Riebeeck's Hedge are highlights.

The **Fragrance garden** features herbs and flowers set out to make appreciating their scents effortless. On a warm day, when the volatile oils are released by the plants, there are some rather over-powering aromas. **The Dell** follows a beautifully shaded path snaking beneath ferns and along a stream. Indigenous South African herbs can be inspected in the **Medicinal Plants** garden, each one identified and used by the Khoi and San peoples in the treatment of a variety of ailments. The plants' uses are identified on plaques, and it seems that most ailments are covered – kidney trouble, rheumatics, coughs, cancer, piles and bronchitis. For a sense of the past, it is worth visiting what is known as **Van Riebeeck's Hedge**. Back in 1660 a hedge of wild almond trees was planted by Van Riebeeck as part of a physical boundary to try and prevent cattle rustling. Segments still remain today within the garden. The **Skeleton Path** can be followed all the way to the summit of Table Mountain. It starts off as a stepped path, but becomes fairly steep near the top. It involves a climb up a rocky waterfall – take special care in the wet season.

● *The café serves over-priced sandwiches and cakes – better value and with far nicer views is the restaurant inside the gardens, just around the corner from the entrance (open until 2200). Another alternative is the picnic hamper service.*

Constantia
Map 1, D3, p246

South of the Botanical Gardens lies Cape Town's most elegant suburb, the verdant area of Constantia and its winelands. This historical district was the first site of wine-making in South Africa, and today it is an attractive introduction to the country's wines, as well as offering some fine examples of Cape Dutch architecture.

There are **five estates** here, of which **Groot Constantia**, T 021-7945128, is the best known and definitely worth a visit. **Buitenverwatchting**, T 021-7945191, is a working estate with an excellent restaurant. **Klein Constantia**, T 021-7945188, is famed for its dessert wine, Vin de Constance, allegedly Napoleon's favourite wine. **Constantia Uitsig**, T 021-7941810, has fine wines and two superb restaurants, Constantia Uitsig and La Colombe. **Steenberg**, T 021-7132211, also offers superb wines as well as having luxurious lodgings, a good restaurant and a golf course.

The old wine estate, **Groot Constantia**, which gave its name to one of the smartest inland residential districts around Cape Town, encapsulates everything that is the old Dutch Cape. The house, outbuildings, museum and vineyards mirror a life and time that were the formative years of Cape Town and South Africa. The Cape Governor Simon van der Stel lived here between 1699 and 1712. He named the estate after Constantia, the daughter of the company official who had granted the land to him. Keen to build a home worthy of the Governor, he checked on every corner and curve with his builders. Before his death, van der Stel planted most of the vines, but it was not until 1778 that the estate became famous for its wines. During this period the estate was unable to meet the demands from Europe, especially France. The magnificent wine cellar behind the main house was designed by the renowned French architect, Louis Thibault. There are two popular restaurants on the estate. A fee is payable at the gate plus a charge to visit the manor house and the old wine cellar.

False Bay

*On the other side of the peninsula lies False Bay, with a string of seaside towns and fishing villages that have a very different feel from the Atlantic Seaboard. Here the main emphasis is on family holidays, and **Muizenberg**, **Simon's Town** and **Kalk Bay** have neither the frenetic pace nor the spectacular landscape of the Atlantic Seaboard. This can mean that they can seem rather twee compared to the slick pace of Cape Town's major haunts, but they also offer excellent beaches and are far more laid back – although the towns are far from quiet during peak season. The main attraction here is the warm water; temperatures can be as much as 8°C higher than at Camps Bay or*

Clifton. While Muizenberg has the finest beach and Simon's Town the best facilities, Kalk Bay is the most enjoyable spot, busy with cafés and antique shops and with a tiny working harbour selling fresh fish straight off the boats. In spring there is the added advantage of seeing calving **whales** in False Bay, with good numbers of Southern Right, humpback and bryde whales.

▶▶ *See Sleeping p125, Eating and drinking p152*

The Metro train line runs to Simon's Town, as do trains. Trains leave approximately every 30 mins. The last train back leaves at Mon-Fri, 2029, Sat, 2019, Sun, 2059, but check. The Golden Arrow runs a bus service to and from Adderley St: information, T 021-9378800. There are two routes across the mountainous spine linking the roads which hug the coast around the peninsula. The most scenic route however is to follow the M65 along the coast from the Atlantic Seaboard to False Bay.

Sights

Muizenberg
Map 1, F4, p246

Travelling out from the city centre, this is the first settlement you reach on False Bay. It is one of the best-known resorts in the peninsula, and has always been a popular bathing spot. The town and its seafront have become rundown and tacky, but the beach itself is a beautiful, vast stretch of powder white sand sloping gently to the water. It is safe for swimming as there is no backwash, and it is easy for surfers.

Muizenberg was first propelled to the forefront of popularity when **Cecil Rhodes** bought a cottage here in 1899. Many other wealthy and famous people followed, building some fine Victorian and Edwardian cottages along today's back streets. Rudyard Kipling, a frequent visitor, wrote about the white sands of Muizenberg in one of his poems. **Sunrise Beach**, 2 km to the east, is the most popular spot today. Behind **West Beach** is a large red and white striped pavilion built in the 1970s, a fun fair, mini golf, fast food outlets, and a collection of distinctive, colourful private bathing huts, reproductions of those built here in the 19th century.

The walk along the main street towards St James is known locally as the **Historic Mile** and will take you past a number of interesting historic buildings. Some of these are national monuments, but not all are open to the public – a few are still private homes. The first building of note is the **Station building**, a fine example of art deco architecture built in 1912.

There are several **paths** leading from the back of the town into the Kalk Bay Mountains and the Silvermine Nature Reserve.

St James
Map 1, G3, p247

Just beyond Muizenberg lies the more upmarket resort of St James, an appealing village with characteristic brightly coloured bathing huts lined along its shore. The village is named after a Roman Catholic Church which was built here in 1854 to save Catholics having to travel as far as Simon's Town to attend services – interestingly, some of the early settlers were Catholic Filipino fishermen. There is a small sheltered beach and reasonable surf off Danger Beach. Several readers have recommended the tidal pool as a safe place for a swim. During the week all is quiet, but at the weekend this is a popular spot and you'll have trouble finding a parking spot; it's best to take the metro train. St James is also a suitable starting point for a hike in the excellent **Silvermine Nature Reserve**. A path starts on Boyes Drive and climbs up through the Spes Bona Forest to Tartarus Cave. The views alone are worth the hike (see below for further details).

Kalk Bay
Map 1, G3, p247

Kalk Bay is one of the most attractive settlements on False Bay and a great spot to relax for a day or two. The town is named after the lime kilns which produced *kalk* from shells in the 17th century. An important local product, the lime created the white-walled appearance of many new houses in the Cape, especially amongst the Bo-Kaap community. Until the arrival of the railway in 1883, the local fishermen hunted whales, seals and small fish. Today it remains a fishing harbour, worked mainly by a coloured community which somehow escaped the Group Areas Act under apartheid. It is one of the few remaining coloured settlements on the peninsula.

Main Road is an appealing spot, lined with antique shops and art galleries, and the beach is sandy and safe for swimming, with a couple of tidal pools for children to explore. Between June and July the harbour is busy for the season for snoek, one of the most plentiful local fish harvests. Look out for the returning deep sea fishing boats around the middle of the day, as there's a daily impromptu quayside auction. You can buy a variety of fresh fish at the counters and an extra R3 get them to gut them for you too. Another attraction is **Seal Island**; cruises are run from the harbour by *Captain Rob's Tours*, T 021-7885261. The island is an important breeding ground for birds and seals, the latter attracting hungry great white sharks. You should also look out for the **Holy Trinity Church** on the Main Road. It has a thatched roof, but its appeal is the windows, considered to be some of the finest in the Cape. On Quarterdeck Road is a tiny mosque built in the 1800s.

Two of the **footpaths** from the Silvermine Nature Reserve start and end on Boyes Drive behind Kalk Bay harbour and railway station. These are the paths along Echo valley and Spes Bona valley. It is in fact possible to make a circular hike by walking up Echo valley to a natural depression known as the 'amphitheatre'. Cross over to Kalk Bay Mountain (516 m), and return down Spes Bona valley. At

★ **Hikes**

the end of the valley you will meet a gravel road; if descending, turn right when you meet this road. Allow at least four hours.

Clovelly
Map 1, G3, p247

Continuing along the main road, the next settlement you reach is Clovelly, tucked between the waters of False Bay and the mountains of the Silvermine Reserve. Along the main street are several shops and places to have a snack. Anyone visiting from the west country in Britain might be interested to know that this community is named after the village in Devon. Golf enthusiasts should head a little way inland for the *Clovelly Country Club*. In order to use the golf course (18 holes) or eat in the delightful restaurant you need to take out temporary membership. The course itself has very narrow fairways and is considered to be quite difficult.

Silvermine Nature Reserve
Access into the reserve is between sunrise and sunset, see overpage for getting there details; 1 Sep-31 Mar, 0800-1900; 1 Apr-31 Aug, 0800-1800. Map 1, F3, p246

This is a popular local reserve, but not often visited by overseas visitors. Table Mountain and Cape Point tend to dominate the open-air attractions, and rightly so, but this reserve is well worth a visit if you enjoy hiking, and are hankering after tremendous views across False Bay and the Atlantic Ocean from the high peaks.

The reserve encompasses, like much of the Cape, one of the oldest floral kingdoms in the world. Over 900 rare and endangered species have been recorded in the mountains. In addition to the plants there are a couple of patches of indigenous forest in the Spes Bona and Echo valleys. Ornithologists should look out for black eagles, ground woodpeckers, orange-breasted sunbirds and rock kestrels. If you're extremely lucky, you may also come across small shy mammals such as lynx, porcupine and various species of mongoose.

The reserve is split into two sections by the Ou Kaapseweg Road as it crosses the Kalk Bay Mountains – the eastern sector and western sector. There is no public transport along this road. By car you can either approach from the Cape Town side or from Noordhoek and Fish Hoek. A variety of footpaths from Muizenberg, St James, Kalk Bay and Chapman's Peak Drive all lead into the reserve and make a pleasant day trip from Cape Town.

Fish Hoek
Map 1, G3, p247

Fish Hoek is one of the most conservative settlements on the coast, not least as the sale of alcohol is famously prohibited here. It does, however, have a fine beach, perhaps the best for swimming along the coast. It stretches right across the Fish Hoek valley – swimming is safe at the southern end of the bay, but avoid the northern end where a small river enters the sea, as there is the danger of quicksand. From mid-August, there is a good chance of catching a glimpse of whales from here. The valley which stretches behind the town joins with Noordhoek beach on the Atlantic coast. In recent geological times this was flooded and all the lands towards Cape Point were in fact an island.

Peers Cave, inland from the Country Club, is a well-known rock shelter where six fossilized human skeletons were discovered in 1927, dated at over 10,000 years old. There are also some paintings on the walls, and it is now a national monument. From the police station it is about 45 minutes' walk to the cave, crossing ancient sand dunes which are further evidence of the change in sea level.

Simon's Town
Map 1, I3, p247

This is perhaps the prettiest town on False Bay, with a pleasant atmosphere and numerous old buildings dating from Victorian times along the Main Street. If you want a break from Cape Town, this makes for an excellent alternative base from which to explore the Southern Peninsula. There is a wide choice of accommodation.

The town is fairly quiet for most of the year but becomes very busy with families during the summer school holidays. Whenever you visit, take some time to wander up the hill away from the main road – the quiet, bougainvillea-bedecked houses and cobbled streets with their sea views are a lovely retreat from the busy beaches. The main swimming spot is **Seaforth Beach**, not far from Boulders. To get there, turn off St George's Road into Seaforth Road after passing the navy block to the left. The beach is the second on the right, on Kleintuin Road. A little further towards Cape Point are two other popular bathing beaches, **Windmill** and **Fisherman's**. The swimming is safe, but there is no surf due to offshore rocks which protect the beach. Look out for some giant pots, a legacy from whaling days, when they were used for melting whale blubber.

! South Africa's 'Unofficial National Flower' is the plastic carrier bag. Such huge numbers can be seen snagged in every tree and fence in the city, that there are plans to make them illegal.

Diving is a very popular activity around the Cape Peninsula. See Sports, p204 for outfits. There is a 9-hole, 18 tee, links course on the seafront, just by the turning for Boulders Beach. This is a narrow course and is a real test for anyone not used to playing in very windy conditions. See Sports, p201.

Heritage Museum, on King George Way, is an excellent museum which faithfully charts the history of the Muslim community in Simon's Town. The town was designated a "white" area during the Group Areas Act and over 7,000 people classified as coloured were relocated. The Amlay family were the last to be forcibly removed from Simon's Town – today the Muslim community has all but disappeared here, although there is still an attractive working mosque up behind Main Road. The exhibition in Heritage House consists mainly of pictures and artefacts dating back to the turn of the century. There is a traditional bridal chamber, with wedding clothes and a display in the Hadj room. Zainab Davidson is the co-founder of the Nourul Islam Historical Society and started the museum. There are also Mosque and Karamat tours.

There are several easy-going **hikes** just behind Simon's Town in the mountains. Close to the railway station is a track referred to as Redhill Path, which actually leads up over Redhill to the village of Scarborough on the Atlantic Coast. You'll need to make arrangements for someone to drive around and collect you from the far side. Far less ambitious, but still as rewarding with the views on offer, is the path known as Klawer Steps. This route starts from the end of Barnard Street, which is off Runciman Drive. At the other end of town, behind the school by Seaforth Beach, you can begin a two-hour walk along an old mule track to a blockhouse which overlooks the harbour. To find it, turn off the main road into Harrington Road and then take a left into Jan Smuts Drive. The mule track is near the far end to the right.

A number of **boat trips** to the Cape of Good Hope originate from Simon's Town harbour. Taking a trip from here allows views of the spectacular coastline and its hinterland from a different

★ Boulders Beach

This beach is home to a colony of African penguins. They take little notice of visitors, swimming and braying around the sunbathers.

angle. In addition to straightforward sightseeing tours, there are several options for viewing bird life, seals and whales during the right season. The advantages in joining a boat tour from Simon's Town as opposed to the V & A Waterfront or Hout Bay is the view of the Hottentots Holland Mountains and False Bay and the waters in False Bay are less rough than those on the Atlantic side. Also, the whole experience is far more relaxed than the large crowds around the V & A Waterfront. See Boat operators, p25.

Whale watching season starts in October. Rules surrounding trips to the see the whales are very stringent, and only one boat a year is given a permit to run whale-watching cruises. These change every year, so it is best to contact the very helpful and informative Publicity Association, T 021-7862436, pensimon@yebo.co.za

★ Boulders Beach
Map 1, I3, p247

About 2 km south of Simon's Town is Boulders, a lovely series of little sandy coves surrounded by huge boulders (hence the name). It is a peaceful spot, safe for swimming and gently shelving, making it good for children. The real attraction here, however, is the colony of African penguins that live and nest between the boulders. Boulders Coastal Park has been created to protect the little creatures, and their numbers have flourished. Bizarrely, they take little notice of their sunbathing neighbours and happily go about their business of swimming, waddling and braying (their characteristic braying was the reason they were, until recently, known as Jackass penguins). The best time to see large numbers is just before sunset, when they return from a day's feeding at sea. Now that the beach is a protected area, there is a R10 admission charge, which is well worth it to get close to the penguins – but avoid the nesting areas. The first cove gets very busy with families at weekends and during school holidays. Walk along the boardwalk or crawl under the rocks on one side of the beach to get to a more peaceful spot.

This is the last easy access to the sea on this side of the peninsula. Beyond Partridge Point the main road cuts into the hillside, and access to the beach is via steep footpaths. **Miller's Point** is one of the few remaining beaches to levy a small entrance fee. Gates close at 2000. There is a large caravan site here plus a picnic area and a restaurant. The road climbs above the sea before rounding the mountains by Smitswinkel Bay. On a clear day you can look back to a perfect view of the cliffs plunging into the sea. A short distance from the shore is the Cape of Good Hope Nature Reserve entrance.

Rondevlei Nature Reserve

T 021-7062404. *0800-1700. Small fee. From Cape Town take the M5, Prince George Dr, turn left into Victoria Rd in Grassy Park, and then right into Fisherman's Walk, about 17 km from the town centre, 6 km from Muizenberg. Map 1, E4, p246*

Despite being surrounded by suburban sprawl this sanctuary is one of the best bird-watching spots close to Cape Town. The 120-km reserve was originally established to protect the birdlife and the coastal *fynbos* (low lying shrubs). Today it is an important environmental education centre for local schools. Only the northern shore of the lake is open to the public. There is a path which follows the vlei's (lake/swamp) edge, along which there are two lookout towers equipped with telescopes. There are several hides along the water's edge, and cuts within the reeds allow views across the water. The best time to visit the reserve is January-March when many European migrants can be seen. Over 200 bird species have been recorded, this figure includes rare visitors, on a good day the visitor should be able to see more than 65 species. There are a few small shy mammals in the reserve, plus a small population of hippopotamus.

Jackass penguins

This flightless sea bird is only found on the coast of southern Africa. Once they nested in guano burrows, today concrete piping can provide the necessary shelter. In the 1930s estimates put their population at over one million birds, today less than 110,000 penguins are left. This considerable decline in the population has been put down to commercial fishing competing with their food stocks and the collection of their eggs for food. They eat sardines, maasbanker, anchovy and squid. Boulders Beach and Bird Island, further along the coast, are the only places where they can be seen nesting on the mainland. These are some of the smaller penguins, but you won't get a better view unless you go to Antarctica or the Falkland Islands.

Tokai Forest

Donation. Take the M3 out of town towards the Southern Suburbs. Before Muizenberg, turn right into Tokai Street, for and follow the signs for Tokai Manor House. Map 1, E3, p246

Tokai was set up as a forest nursery in 1883 to try and stem the destruction of forest reserves, and start a programme of conservation and reforestation. It is within the lands of an old wine estate, Tokai Homestead (1795), named after a wine region of Hungary. This is one of the few areas where the region's indigenous forest and some wildlife have been fully protected and preserved. The arboretum contains 40 tree species – there are two walking trails in the forest, and horse riding and picnicking are possible in the low-lying section of the forest. One of the designated walks is marked by white 'elephants', a trail which leads you up the mountain through the forest to Elephant's Eye cave.

Listings

Museums and galleries

- **Bertram House** A Georgian house decorated with 19th-century British furnishings, p34.
- **Bo-Kaap Museum** A museum dedicated to Cape Malays, p53.
- **Castle of Good Hope** Home to three museums: William Fehr Collection, Secunde's House and a military museum, p44.
- **District Six Museum** Powerful and moving exhibitions giving a fascinating insight into apartheid, p45.
- **Heritage Museum** An excellent museum that charts the history of the Muslim community in Simon's Town, p81.
- **Holocaust Centre** This museum shockingly and intelligently examines the Holocaust, p38.
- **Irma Stern Museum** Displays of the artists work, p70.
- **Jewish Museum** A rich and rare collection of items depicting the history of the Jewish community on the Cape, p35.
- **Koopmans-De Wet House** A restored house offering an interesting insight into the lives of cultured society in early 19th-century Cape Town, p48.
- **National Gallery** Houses local and international art, p38.
- **Rust en Vreugd** A restored 18th-century mansion with six galleries containing works of art depicting the history of the Cape, p39.
- **Slave Lodge** This museum, which started life as a lodge for slaves, surprisingly celebrates colonialism rather than focusing on slave trade although there are plans afoot to reverse the emphasis, p41.
- **South Africa Museum and Planetarium** The cities most established museum specializing in natural history, ethnography and archaeology, p34.
- **South African Missionary House Museum** The oldest mission church in Cape Town now has a permanent display of the work throughout the Cape, p52.

The Winelands 89

The Winelands is South Africa's oldest and most beautiful wine-producing area, a fertile series of valleys quite unlike the rest of the Western Cape. Despite producing less than a third of South Africa's wines, it is the Cape's biggest attraction after Cape Town. Its appeal is simple: the chance to sample world-class wines in a historical and superbly scenic setting.

The Whale Coast 106

The Whale Coast, a couple of hour's drive from Cape Town, lives up to its title from July to November, when large numbers of whales seek out the sheltered bays along the coast for breeding. Hermanus, a well-developed and pleasant seaside resort, is the most popular spot, but whales can be seen all along Walker's Bay.

The Winelands

This was the first region after Cape Town to be settled, and the towns of Stellenbosch, Paarl and Franschhoek are some of the oldest in South Africa. Today their streets are lined with beautiful Cape Dutch and Georgian houses, although the real architectural gems are the manor houses on the wine estates. While the wine industry flourished during the 18th and 19th centuries, the farmers built grand homesteads with cool wine cellars. Most of these can be visited during a trip to a vineyard – a few have even been converted into luxury hotels. Consider hiring a car. On a long day you could visit all the wineland towns and still catch sunset at Cape Point.

Stellenbosch is 46 km from Cape Town and is served by the Metro railway (1 hr). The N2 takes you along the northern fringes of the Cape Flats. The R310 left turning is the quickest route to the town, the R44 is an alternative route to the heart of the area.

Stellenbosch

Stellenbosch, the centre of the Winelands, is the oldest and most attractive town in the region, and one of South Africa's finest. The town itself is a pleasing mix of architectural styles – Cape Dutch, Georgian, Regency and Victorian houses line broad streets dappled with shade from centuries-old oak trees, and roadside furrows still carry stream water to the gardens. It is the most pleasant of the Wineland towns, has several good museums, a good nightlife thanks to the university, and is also a good base for visiting the wine estates. The town offers two approaches to sightseeing: walking around the town centre viewing public buildings or going on a wine tour, visiting one of five co-operative wineries and 23 private cellars. Spend a couple of days in Stellenbosch and you'll get to do both.

▶▶ *See Sleeping p127, Eating and drinking p155 and Map 8 p256*

Dorp Street

Gallery and museum. *Mon-Fri 0900-1245, 1400-1700, Sat 1000-1300, 1400-1700.*

Dorp Street, which runs east-west in the southern part of town, is one of the finest in Stellenbosch. A walk from Libertas Parva to the Theological College takes you through the oldest parts of town and past some of the best preserved old buildings. The **Rembrandt** van Rijn Art Gallery is housed in the beautifully restored Libertas Parva, a classic H-shaped manor house built in 1783. It houses a small collection of 20th-century South African art, including paintings by Irma Stern, see also p70.

The most famous shop in Stellenbosch is as much a tourist attraction as an ongoing business. **Oom Samie se Winkel** (Uncle Sammy's Shop), 84 Dorp Street, has been trading since 1791. The first owner traded in meat, but the shop became famous between 1904 and 1944 when the store was owned and run by Samuel Johannes Volsteedt. He stocked virtually everything you could need, and was known throughout the town. Today the shop still sells a wide range of goods and it has retained its pre-war character with items hanging from all corners and old cabinets full of bits and pieces.

On the corner of Dorp Street and Strand, is the **Stellenryck Wine Museum** which houses an assorted collection of old wine making tools and some furniture. Look out for the giant wine press outside.

Of particular note on Dorp Street are the **town houses** just past the junction with Helderberg Street. Numbers 153, Hauptfleisch House, 155, Bakker House, 157, Loubser House, and 159, Saxenhof, are regarded as the best-preserved street façades in old Stellenbosch.

! Stellenbosch was the first European settlement in the interior of Southern Africa when in November 1679 Simon van der Stel left Cape Town to explore the hinterland.

Branching off from Dorp is **Drostdy Street**, dominated by a building with a tall tower known as Utopia. Also in this street is the town church, the **Moederkerk**, actually the fourth incarnation of the town church. The current steeple church was designed by Carl Otto Hagen, and built in 1862. Inside it is worth admiring the pulpit, built by craftsmen who came from the Netherlands with their own timber. It has nine coloured stained glass windows.

Botanical Gardens

Off Neethling St *Mon Fri 0900-1630, Sat 0900-1100.*

The Botanical Gardens are part of the University of Stellenbosch. There is a fine collection of ferns, orchids and bonsai trees. One of the more unusual plants to look out for is the *Welwitschis* from the Namib Desert.

Village Museum

Ryneveld St, **T** 021-8872902, www.museums.org.za/stellmus *Mon-Sat 0930-1700, Sun 1400-1700. R10.*

The Village Museum is the most interesting sight in Stellenbosch. The complex currently spreads over two blocks in the oldest part of town. There are four houses, each representing a different period of the town's history. The oldest of these is Schreuderhuis (1709), one of the earliest houses to be built in Stellenbosch. The simple furniture and collection of household objects are all of the same period. Blettermanhuis (1789) is a perfect example of what has come to be regarded as a typical H-shaped Cape Dutch home. The furnishings are those of a wealthy household between 1750-80. The third building in the museum to have been restored is Grosvenor House (1803), in Drostdy Street. This is an excellent example of the two-storeyed town house that once dominated the streets of Cape Town. The fourth and final house is the fussy OM Bergh House (1870), which once had a thatched roof.

The Braak

The Braak, at the western end of Church Street, is where much of the town's activity takes place. This is the original village green, and one-time military parade ground. On the western edge by Market Street is the VOC-Kruithuis, or Powder House, built in 1777 as a weapons store. Today it is a military museum, open only in the mornings. The bell tower was added at a much later date. Two churches overlook the Braak. The first is Rhenish Church, built in 1832 as a training school for coloureds and slaves, and which has a very fine pulpit. The other is St Mary's-on-the-Braak, an Anglican church completed in 1852.

Stellenbosch Wine Route

This was the first wine route to open in South Africa, in April 1971. It was the idea of three local farmers: Neil Joubert, Frans Malan and Spatz Sperling. It has been hugely successful, attracting tens of thousands of visitors every year, and today the membership comprises 42 private cellars. It is possible to taste and buy wines at all of them, and the cellars can arrange for your purchases to be delivered internationally. Many of the estates have developed excellent restaurants as well as providing very popular picnic lunches – at weekends it is advisable to book if you wish to eat at a particular place.

Delaire

T 021-8851756, www.delairewinery.co.za *Mon-Sat, 1000-1700, Sun, 1000-1600. Cellar tours by appointment only. Map 8, E3, p256*

Delaire is a small estate which has managed to produce some very high-standard wines. During the last five years their Chardonnay has been a popular export label. On a clear day visitors are rewarded with views of the Simonsberg Mountains.

Delheim

T 021-8822033, www.delheim.com *Sales and tastings Mon-Fri, 0830-1700, Sat, 0900-1500, Sun, 1100-1500 (Oct-April only). Cellar tours Mon-Fri, 1030 and 1430, Sat, 1030. Map 8, D3, p256*

Delheim is one of the more commercially orientated estates and may be a little too impersonal for some visitors. However the *Vintner's Platter Garden Restaurant* has a beautiful setting with views towards Cape Town and Table Mountain. Tastings are conducted in a cool downstairs cellar.

Hartenberg

Off Bottelary Rd, **T** 021-8652541, www.hartenbergestate.com *Mon-Fri, 0900-1700; Sat, 0900-1500; closed Sun. Map 8, D2, p256*

Hartenberg is an old estate, founded in 1692. It is currently privately owned with a wide variety of red and white wines produced from 16 different grape varieties. During the summer, lunches are served in the shade and peace of the gardens; come winter the tasting room doubles up as a restaurant with warming log fires. Their Semillion blended white has been well reviewed.

Neethlingshof

T 021-8838988, www.neethlingshof.co.za *Mon-Fri, 0900-1700/ 1900; Sat and Sun, 1000-1600/1800. Cellar tours by appointment. Vineyard tours 1100, 1200 and 1300 (Nov-Apr only). Map 8, E2, p256*

Neethlingshof, a traditional Cape Dutch H-style homestead, houses the *Lord Neethling* restaurant. The approach to the manor house is via a unique stone pine avenue. The new owners have invested in the latest cellar technology and replanted the vineyards – the results have won awards throughout the last decade. Ones to look out for are the Cabernet Sauvignon '95 and the Lord Neethling Pinotage '97.

▶ Grape expectations

South Africa has become one of the world's major wine producers, and although not yet as successful as those of Australia, standards are improving rapidly. A number of Cape wines are excellent and most are very good value.

The Cape's wine industry was started in earnest by Simon van der Stel in 1679. Previously, vines had been grown by Van Riebeeck in Company's Garden and in the area known today as the suburb of Wynberg. As the early settlers moved inland and farms were opened up in the sheltered valleys, more vines were planted. Van der Stel produced the first quality wines on Constantia estate in Cape Town, but a great boost to the fledgling industry was the arrival of the French Huguenots in 1688, and for a while Constantia's wines were in demand in France. Indeed, a little-known fact is that the first vineyards of the Cape were planted before those in the Bordeaux region of France.

The industry received a further boost in 1806 when the English, at war with France, started to import South African wines. However, under apartheid the wine industry suffered, as sanctions hindered exports and the Kooperatieve Wijnbouwers Vereniging (KWV) controlled prices and productions quotas. The KWV has since lost much of its power, allowing the industry to experiment and expand.

The modern wine industry has developed out of the need to find better quality grapes. The Hanepoort grape proved to be too delicate to travel. These days, hundreds of varieties are cultivated in the Cape. Each river valley produces its own distinct wine, using the grape best suited to the local climatic conditions. The region around Stellenbosch remains the heartland of the industry, but you are likely to see vines growing in the Cape wherever there is a guaranteed supply of irrigated water.

Saxenburg

T 021-9036113, www.saxenburg.co.za *Mon-Fri, 0900-1700; Sat, 0900-1600; Sun, 1100-1700 (Sep-Oct only). Map 8, E1, p256*

Saxenburg, off the M12, is close to Kuils River. It is only in the last decade that it has been developed into a showpiece on the Wine Route. The estate only produces a small number of cases each year, but some of the Private Collection is very good. The *Guinea Fowl* restaurant attracts most of the visitors.

Uittyk

T 021-8844416, F8844717. *Mon-Fri, 0900-1700, Sat, 0090-1230, closed Sun. Map 8, E1, p256*

Uittyk is a very fine wine estate but not a member of the Stellenbosch Wine Route. A fine Georgian-style manor house dating from 1712 is the centrepiece. Wine tastings are conducted in a relaxed and friendly atmosphere. A visit here is highly recommended. Two of the finer wines on offer are their Sauvignon Blanc '97/98 and Cabernet/Shiraz '94.

★ Vergelegen Estate

T 021-8471344. *0930-1600. R7, fee includes wine tasting and a cellar tour. Cellar tours: 1030, 1130 and 1430, closed Sun. Map 8, G3, p256*

Vergelegen Estate is one of the Cape's finest estates, and you should allow several hours for a visit. The highlight is a visit to the magnificent manor house and its octagonal garden. The house is full of period furniture and paintings, similar to the collection at Groot Constantia. Between October and April you can have an alfresco lunch overlooking a collection of rose bushes. The modern cellars are buried on Rondekop Hill, overlooking the estate – there are good views from here of the mountains and False Bay.

Franschhoek

This is undoubtedly one of the most pleasant Wineland villages, but the reality is that most of the attractions here have been created to serve the tourist industry. The outlying wine estates all have their individual appeal, but the village itself is mostly restaurants and touristy shops. However, many of the restaurants are very good – a visit to Franschhoek should always include a good meal.

▸▸ *See Sleeping, p129, Eating and drinking, p157 and Map 8, p256*

Franschhoek is 71 km from Cape Town (via N1). There is no public transport from Cape Town to Franschhoek. Franschhoek is 26 km from Paarl.

Huguenot Memorial Museum and Monument collection

Lambrecht St. *Mon-Fri 0900-1700, Sat 0900-1300, 1400-1700, Sun 1400-1700. Small fee.*

This museum is housed in two buildings either side of Lambrecht Street. The main building, to the left of the Huguenot Monument, is modelled on a house designed by the French architect, Louis Michel Thibault, built in 1791 at Kloof Street, Cape Town. The displays inside trace the history of the Huguenots in South Africa and their way of life. There are some fine collections of furniture, silverware and family Bibles, but little to hold one's attention for very long. One of the roles of the museum today is to maintain an up-to-date register of families and their children, so that future generations will be able to trace their ancestors.

Next door to the museum is the unattractive Huguenot Monument, a highly symbolic memorial built to mark 250 years since the first Huguenots settled in the Cape. It is set in a peaceful rose garden with the rugged Franschhoek Mountains as a backdrop. The architect was JC Jongens and the central female figure is the work of C Steynberg. The three arches represent the Trinity, and the golden sun and cross on top are the Sun of Righteousness and the Cross of Christian Faith. In front of the arches is a statue of a woman with a Bible in her right hand and a broken chain in her left, symbolizing freedom from religious oppression. If you look closely at the globe you can see several objects carved into the southern tip of Africa: a Bible, harp, spinning wheel and a sheaf of corn and the vine. These represent different aspects of the Huguenots' life, respectively their faith, their art and culture, their industry and their agriculture. The final piece of the memorial, the curved colonnade, represents tranquillity and spiritual peace after the problems they had faced in France.

Franschhoek Wine Route

All the vineyards lie along the Franschhoek valley, making it one of the most compact wine routes in the region. What makes this such a rewarding route is that several estates have opened their own excellent restaurants and five also offer luxury overnight accommodation. All the valley's wine can be tasted at the Franschhoek Vineyards Co-operative, located on the right just before you enter the village when approaching from Stellenbosch.

Boschendal
T 021-8704203, www.boschendalwines.co.za *Mon-Sat, 0830-1630; Nov-Apr, Sun, 0930-1230. Vineyard tours 1030 and 1130, by appointment. Map 8, D4, p256*

Boschendal estate has been growing wine for 300 years and is today one of the most popular estates in the region. Most of the wine produced on the estate is white; their sparkling wines are highly regarded. The wine cellar has been converted into the excellent Boschendal restaurant which serves a superb buffet lunch.

Wine class
Many private wine cellars have opened up their doors to visitors offering wine tastings in beautiful surroundings. Many are historial attractions in themselves and well worth visiting.

Mont Rochelle

T 021-8763000, montrochelle@wine.co.za *Mon-Sat, 1100-1700; Sun, 1100-1300. Cellar tours Mon-Fri 1100, 1230, 1500. Map 8, E6, p256*

This estate has one of the most attractive settings in the region, with beautiful views of the valley. Graham and Lyn de Villiers, eighth generation descendants of the original Huguenot Jacques de Villiers, have redeveloped the winery and re-fitted the 150-year-old Victorian cellar.

La Motte

T 021-8763119, www.la-motte.co.za *Mon-Fri, 0900-1630; Sat, 0900-1200. Cellar tours by appointment. Map 8, D5, p256*

This estate was built in 1752 and the grand old cellars, worth a visit for alone, are now used for wine tasting. All the wines are made and bottled on the estate. As a relatively small producer, only 15,000 cases per annum, the estate has managed to create some excellent wines. Look out for their Millennium '97.

L'Ormarins

T 021-8741026. *Appointment only Mon-Fri, 0900-1630; Sat, 0900-1200. Map 8, D4, p256*

L'Ormarins vineyard has a beautiful setting on the slopes of the Drakensteinberge. The present homestead was built in 1811 – from its grand marble halls and staircases you look out across an ornamental pond and neat mature gardens. The other notable attraction is the original wine cellar; this has been carefully restored and now houses a set of giant wine vats. L'Ormarins has won a large number of medals and trophies over the last 25 years.

Four Passes route

One of the popular recommended day drives from Cape Town is known as the Four Passes route. This takes you through the heart of the Winelands, and as the title suggests over four mountain passes. The first stop on the drive is Stellenbosch. From here you take the R310 towards Franschhoek. Driving up out of Stellenbosch you cross the first pass, **Helshoogte Pass**. After 17 km you reach a T-junction with the R45: a left turn would take you to Paarl, 12 km, but the route continues to the right. This is a very pleasant drive up into the Franschhoek Valley. The road follows a railway line and for a part the Berg River. After passing through Franschhoek, take a left in front of the Huguenot Monument and climb out of the valley via the **Franschhoek Pass**. This pass was built along the tracks formed by migrating herds of game centuries earlier, and was originally known as the Olifantspad (elephant's path). One of the more surprising aspects of this drive is the change in vegetation once you cross the lip of the pass, 520 m above the level of Franschhoek. As the road winds down towards Theewaterskloof Dam you pass through a dry valley full of scrub vegetation and fynbos – gone are the fertile fruit farms and vineyards. Take a right across the dam on the R321 towards Grabouw and Elgin. The route continues across the Theewaterskloof Dam and then climbs **Viljoens Pass**, the third of four. To the right lies the Hottentots Holland Nature Reserve, a popular hiking region. The country around here is an important apple growing region. The fourth and the most spectacular pass is **Sir Lowry's Pass**, which crosses the Hottentots Holland Mountains.

Paarl

While Paarl is home to two of South Africa's better-known wine estates, KWV and Nederburg, the town itself is not as interesting as Stellenbosch nor as fashionable as Franschhoek. All of the attractions

and restaurants are strung out along Main Street at the base of
Paarl Mountain. When the first European, Abraham Gabbema, saw
the mountain in October 1657 it had just rained; the granite domes
sparkled in the sunlight and he named the mountains paarl (pearl)
and diamandt (diamond). The town grew in a random fashion
along an important wagon route to Cape Town. Several old buildings
survive, but they are spread out rather than concentrated in a few
blocks like Stellenbosch. Paarl is also a delightful place to watch an
international cricket match in a peaceful rural setting. A good braai
and some fine local wines make for a perfect day out.

▸▸ See Sleeping p130, Eating and drinking p159 and Map 8 p256

There are regular trains between Cape Town and Paarl.

Main Street and around
Paarl Museum Mon-Fri 0800-1700. Afrikaans Language Museum
Mon-Fri 0900-1300, 1400-1700.

The 1-km walk along Main Street will take you past most of the
finest buildings in Paarl. Here you'll find one of the oldest buildings, the **Paarl Museum**, at 303 Main Street. This houses a
reasonably diverting collection of Cape Dutch furniture. There is
also a small section outlining Paarl during apartheid, although
the fact that Nelson Mandela spent his final years in prison in Paarl
is barely mentioned. Only a few hundred metres away, in Gideon
Malherbe House, on Pastorie Street, the **Afrikaans Language
Museum** gives a detailed chronicle of the development of the
Afrikaans language and the people involved.

Near Lady Grey Street is **Zeederberg Square**, a 19th-century
square with a fine mix of restored buildings and lively restaurants.

! Paarl is where Nelson Mandela spent his final years in prison.
His first steps of freedom were from Victor Verster Prison,
9 km south of Paarl.

Further south on Main Street is the **Strooidakkerk**, a thatched roof church, consecrated in 1805 and still in use. It stands in a spacious churchyard full of flowers and cypress trees. It was designed by George Küchler – note the gables, a sounding-board to amplify sermons and the fine pulpit. You may have to ask for a key from the church office.

Arboretum

Open during daylight hours. From the Publicity Office go down Market St, cross the river and it is on the right.

On the east bank of the Berg river is the 31-ha arboretum. There are over 700 different species in a total of 4,000 trees. The grounds have been divided into six sections, each containing species from different continents. There are 153 species from Africa, 48 from South America, 93 from North America, 113 from Australasia, 185 from Asia and 81 species from Europe.

● *The best views of the surrounding countryside are from Bretagne Rock; on a clear day you can see False Bay, Table Mountain and all the vineyards.*

Taal Monument

Small fee.

Set high on the slopes of Paarl Mountain amongst granite boulders and indigenous trees stands the Taal Monument – three concrete columns linked by a low curved wall. This is the Afrikaans language monument, inaugurated in October 1975 and designed by Jan van Wijk. Each column represents different influences in the language. The relative heights of each column and the negative connotations associated with them have been the subject of criticism in recent years. From here you have an excellent view across the Berg River valley.

Butterfly World
Klapmuts, **T** 021-8755628. *0900-1700; Jun-Aug, 1000-1600. R15.*

Those with kids in tow may wish to visit Butterfly World, the largest such park in South Africa, with butterflies flying freely in colourful landscaped gardens. Craft shop and tea garden.

Paarl Wine Route

The route was set up in 1984 by local producers to help promote their wines and attract tourists into the area. The programme has been a great success and some of the estates have opened their own restaurants. These are usually very good, but don't expect huge discounts on the wine with your meal. All of the estates have tastings and wine sales on a daily basis. Only the largest estates conduct regular cellar tours.

Boland Kelder
T 021-8726190, boland@wine.co.za *Mon-Fri, 0800-1700; Sat, 0830-1300. Cellar tours by appointment. Map 8, A4, p256*

Boland Kelder estate has an excellent wine cellar, and offers one of the most interesting cellar tours. One of their best wines is the Noble Late Harvest '92, made from the chenin blanc grape.

Fairview Wine Estate
T 021-8632450, fairback@iafrica.com *Wine and cheese sales and tastings Mon-Fri 0800-1700, Sat 0800-1700. Map 8, C3, p256*

This is a popular estate with a rather unusual attraction in the form of a goat tower, a spiral structure home to two pairs of goats. In addition to a variety of very good wines – look out for the popular Goats do Roam and their 2000 Chardonnay – visitors can taste goat and Jersey milk cheeses. The goats are milked each afternoon from 1530 onwards.

Laborie

T 021-8073390, **F** 8071955, grovelj@kwv.co.za *0900-1700. Cellar tours by appointment. Map 8, C4, p256*

Laborie is the easiest cellar to visit as it is close to the centre of town. The vineyard is impressive, developed with tourism in mind. The original Cape Dutch homestead, surrounded by rose bushes, has been turned into a restaurant serving good value buffets or a more fancy à la carte menu. Closed Sunday and Monday evening. There is a lovely tasting terrace, and rolling lawns overlooking the vineyards.

Nederburg

T 021-8623104, www.nederburg.co.za *Mon-Fri, 0830-1700; Sat, 0900-1300 (Nov-Feb). Cellar tours, appointment only. Map 8, B4, p256*

Nederburg is one of the largest and best-known estates in South Africa. Their annual production is in excess of 650,000 cases – the small Paarl estates produce in the region of 3,000 cases. As such a large concern they are involved in much of the research in South Africa to improve the quality of the grape and the vine. Every April the annual Nederburg Auction attracts buyers from all over the world. The best wines compare favourably worldwide; the Cabernet Sauvignon '91 is rated by John Platter as a classic wine.

Sonop Winery

T 021-8872475, sonop@iafrica.com *Map 8, A3, p256*

Sonop Winery is fundamentally different from most in the Winelands as it is community-driven, where the farm workers have a direct input in the running of the business. Proceeds go towards local community projects and schools. They have only recently started tastings, so be sure to phone ahead to check that it's possible. One of the better wines produced here is Winds of Change, an organic Semillon Chardonnay blend.

Villeria

T 021-8822002, villeria@mweb.co.za *Mon-Fri, 0830-1700; Sat, 0830-1300. Cellar tours by appointment. Map 8, D1, p256*

Villeria is highly regarded and produces some of the best wines in the Cape. There are plenty of classic wines to choose from, including the Cru Monro, the Merlot '89 and their Sauvignon Blanc. They no longer conduct cellar tours, but allow 'self-guided' tours.

The Whale Coast

The viewing of whales is naturally the main attraction, however, elsewhere along the coast there are miles of sandy beaches, wrecks to scuba dive, the chance of seeing the great white shark, and the southernmost point in Africa – Cape Agulhas. The most beautiful and exhilarating stretch of coast to drive along is between Gordon's Bay and Hermanus, where the mountains plunge straight into the ocean forming a coastline of steep cliffs, sandy coves, dangerous headland and natural harbours.

Hermanus

Hermanus has grown from a rustic fishing village to a well-known town famous for its superb whale watching. Today it is marketed as the world's best land-based whale watching site, and Walker Bay is host to impressive numbers during calving season (July to November). However, don't expect any private viewings – Hermanus is very popular and has a steady flow of tourists throughout the year, and is especially busy at Christmas. While this means it can get very busy, there is also a good range of accommodation and restaurants. Alternatively, Hermanus is only a few hours from Cape Town, making it an easy day trip from the city.

▸▸ *See Sleeping p131 and Eating and drinking p161*

Hermanus is 120 km from Cape Town (via N2). The easiest way to visit, if you don't have a car, is to travel on the Baz Bus from Cape Town to the Bot River Hotel. The main coach lines travel along the coast.

The **old harbour** is a national monument and a focal point of tourist activities. A ramp leads down the cliff to the old jetty and a group of restored fishermen's cottages, including the museum. The displays are based on the local fishing industry and include models of fish, a whale skeleton, some shark jaws, fish tanks and early pieces of equipment. One of the most interesting features is the recordings of calls between whales. There is also a telescope to watch the whales further out. Outside the museum on the harbour ramp is a collection of small restored fishing boats, the earliest dating from 1855. Also on show are the drying racks for small fish and cement tables which were once used for gutting fish. (*Mon-Sat, 0900-1300, 1400-1700, Sun 1200-1600*). The **new harbour**, to the west of the old harbour in Westcliff, is still a busy fishing port.

There are some good beaches just a short distance in either direction from the town centre. The best beaches to the west are found at Onrus and Vermont. **Grotto Beach** is the largest, best developed and most popular for swimming. The fine white sands stretch beyond the Klein River Lagoon. There are changing facilities, a restaurant and a shop. Slightly closer to the town centre is **Voëlklip Beach**, a little rundown, but with well-kept lawns behind the sand. Conditions are good for swimming and surfing. The most popular spot for surfers is **Kammabaai** next door to Voëlklip Beach. Heading east towards Stanford and Gansbaai are long, open beaches or secluded coves with patches of sand and plenty of rock pools.

A great walk takes you along the **Cliff Path**. It starts at the new harbour in Westcliff and follows the shore all the way round Walker Bay to Grotto Beach, a distance of just over 15 km. Between cliffs the path goes through stands of milkwood trees and takes you around the sandy beaches.

Hermanus Wine Route

Hidden away in the **Hemel-en-Aarde Valley** behind Hermanus is a small collection of vineyards producing some surprisingly good wines, mostly Burgundy varieties based around pinot noir and chardonnay grapes. These smaller and lesser-known wineries are very pleasant to visit since they are rarely crowded and the owners are enthusiastic about their venture. There are three vineyards which are open to the public and have tastings in their cellars. **Hamilton Russell Vineyards** is one of the more picturesque estates. The cellar and tasting room are set beside a small trout lake. (**T** 028-3123595. Closed Sun. Follow the R43 out of Hermanus towards Cape Town, and after 2 km take a right turn marked Caledon, R320; there is a signpost and right turn 5 km along this gravel road.) **Whalehaven Wines** is the newest vineyard in the valley, and all their wines are quite young. The cellars and the production rooms are open to visitors. (**T** 028-3161633. Closed Sun. Take the R320 turning for Caledon as described above. Immediately on the right after turning off the R43.).

Betty's Bay

Heading west towards Strand is this small holiday village, a gem best known to local folk. The village is an untidy collection of holiday homes, but the location is beautiful. At Stoney Point there is a reserve to protect a small breeding colony of **African penguins**, one of the few places where you are guaranteed to see these birds breeding on the mainland. Behind the village are the well-known **Harold Porter Botanic Gardens**, worth a visit if time permits. Along the main beach is another area of protected land, the **HF Verwoerd Coastal Reserve**. Along the beach rare shells are occasionally washed ashore. There is safe swimming close to the kelp beds.

Stanford

This peaceful Victorian village, with its limewashed buildings and slow pace, has become a popular centre amongst artists and craftsfolk. It's a good place to wander around for an hour or two. Several shops and studios are open to visitors. There is also the **Birkenhead Micro-Brewery**, just out of town off the R326 to Caledon. The first beer was served here in September 1998, and already there is tremendous local demand. It is a delicious slow brewed beer using rich malted two-rowed barley and aromatic Hallertau and Saaz hop cones.

Gansbaai

On the eastern end of Walker Bay is Gansbaai, named by fishermen – after a colony of Egyptian geese, *kolganse*, which used to nest in the reeds in the bay – who used the bay to protect themselves against large storms. Today the village is a prosperous fishing harbour with several fish canning factories while at the same time it has managed to retain the character of a small community with strong ties with the tourist industry. Many people from Cape Town have second houses along this coast.

There are some good vantage points for whale watching. A couple of kilometres up the coast at **De Kelders** are some tall cliffs which quickly give way to a large white sand beach. The main reason for coming here is to visit **Dyer Island**, named after Samson Dyer, a black American who lived on the island collecting guano around 1806. Today the island is an important breeding spot for African penguins. On nearby **Geyser Island** there is a huge breeding seal population, and the narrow canal between the island attracts a number of great white sharks, giving it the name of **Shark Alley**. A boat trip here is hugely entertaining – even if you don't see any sharks, there are hundreds of seals and birds. Cage diving to see the sharks is popular here – for those with a diving certificate. However, more recently conservationists have pointed out that these trips can be harmful to the sharks. Firstly, the tour companies feed the sharks clearly interfering with their natural feeding patterns. Secondly, great whites are thought to be beginning to equate humans with food – contrary to popular belief, we do not feature on their usual menu – thus increasing the risk of attacks. If you are considering viewing the sharks off Dyer Island, check with the tourist office which is currently the best company running trips – one peferably partaking in conservation and research into the species. There are two seasons for viewing – low season, October through to mid-January and high season. During low season, operators reckon the probability of viewing is eight days out of ten.

Elim

Further east and inland lies this well-known Moravian mission station. It was founded by German missionaries in 1824 and inhabited only by members of the Moravian church. The settlement name comes from Exodus 15:27, the name given to the spot where the Israelites rested after crossing the Red Sea. To live here you must still be a member of the local church and your livelihood must come from the earth. The whole village has been declared a National Monument, so it is not surprising to find a variety of quaint old buildings still standing and in use. It is interesting but perhaps not worth the journey there alone. To get the most out of a visit contact the tourist bureau, T 028-48806, F 48705, in advance and arrange to have a guide meet you.

Cape Agulhas

Continuing south you reach the southernmost tip of Africa, Cape Agulhas. Although it's great to be able to say you've been there, it is not spectacular and not really worth the drive.

The city centre and surrounds offer an excellent selection of accommodation, from exclusive vineyard estates and fashionable boutique hotels, to cosy seaside guesthouses and trendy backpacker lodges. Accommodation tends to be very good value for money, and with the current exchange rate you can get some excellent bargains, especially out of season. Prices vary considerably, but there's something to suit every budget. A luxurious suite on a historical estate can cost as much as R4,000 a night; a comfortable town hotel should be no more than R1,000, while smaller guesthouses and B&Bs are usually between R300 and R800. Backpacker hostels can be as cheap as R50.

There is no one particular area that visitors usually stay in. Accommodation is spread around the city, with a good range in the centre, along the coasts and in the suburbs. The Winelands and Whale Coast also have plenty on offer. Bear in mind that the Cape is extremely popular, especially over the Christmas period, so be sure to book several months in advance.

R **Sleeping codes**

AL	R1,500 and over	**D**	R180-300
A	R750-1,500	**E**	R90-180
B	R480-750	**F**	less than R90
C	R300-780		

Price of a double room not including service charges or meals

The city centre

Hotels

AL Mount Nelson, 76 Orange St, Gardens, **T** 021-4231000, **F** 4247472. *Map 2, D5, p248* This is *the* luxury hotel with 131 rooms, 28 suites and eight garden cottage suites, although the rooms are outdated. Set in 7-km of its own landscaped parkland, it has a heated swimming pool, tennis courts, squash court, beauty centre and excellent restaurant serving Cape specialities.

A The Cullinan, 1 Cullinan St, Centre, **T** 021-4186920, **F** 4183559, www.thecullinan.co.za *Map 3, F12, p251* Smart, large, upmarket hotel popular with business men. A short walk from the city centre and Waterfront. All the mod cons and good city views.

A-B De Waterkant Lodge & Cottages, 20 Loader St, Bo-Kaap, **T/F** 021-4191097, waterkant@iafrica.com *Map 3, F9, p251* Situated on the edge of Bo-Kaap suburb, 16 luxuriously restored cottages, all have two double rooms, modern kitchens, TV, a/c, telephone. Serviced daily, close to the shops and restaurants. Access to swimming pool, jacuzzi and sauna. Good value. Airport transfer.

A **Kensington Place**, 38 Kensington Gardens, Higgovale, **T** 021-4244744, **F** 4241810, www.kensingtonplace.co.za *Map 2, G2, p248* Stylish boutique hotel in a quiet, leafy area. Small and well run with excellent service. Beautiful rooms, individually styled with views over the city, bar, small pool and deck, excellent restaurant.

A **No 1 Chesterfield**, 1 Chesterfield Rd, Oranjezicht, **T** 021-4617383, **F** 4614688. *Map 2, H4, p248* Eight rooms, each decorated in a different theme: Cape Dutch, French, Zulu and West African. Swimming pool, quiet setting, evening meals on request.

A **Villa Belmonte**, 33 Belmont Av, Oranjezicht, **T** 021-4621576, **F** 4621579. *Map 2, H5, p248* Eight rooms, TV, an award-winning luxury Italian-style villa. Shady veranda with views of Table Mountain, meals by arrangement, swimming pool, smart and elegant set up.

B **Ikhaya Guest Lodge**, Dunkley Sq, Gardens, **T** 021-4618880, **F** 4618889, www.ikhayalodge.co.za *Map 2, D7, p249* A tasteful development a short distance from the city centre with 11 double rooms, five apartments for self-catering guests. Full of character thanks to the natural woods, African fabrics and recycled decorations (the bedside lamps are made from old ginger beer bottles).

B **Tudor Hotel**, Greenmarket Sq, Centre, **T** 021-4241335, **F** 4231198, www.tudorhotel@iafrica.co.za *Map 2, A7, p249* 30 rooms, a small welcoming hotel which hasn't lost its character through redevelopment, all the rooms have a worn but homely feel. The restaurant, bar and café have a continental atmosphere and serve good food, ideal location for exploring the city centre, covered parking, good value, booking advised.

B **Underberg Guest House**, 6 Tamboerskloof Rd, **T** 021-4262262, **F** 4244059, underberg@netactive.co.za *Map 2, C3, p248* Smart old corner house with decorative iron balconies, nine spacious rooms with en suite bathrooms, TV and mini bar, full English breakfast, laundry service, secure parking, convenient for city centre, friendly and helpful owners.

C Ambleside Guest House, 11 Forest Rd, Oranjezicht, **T** 021-4652503, **F** 4653814, guest **T** 021-4655281. *Map 2, H4, p248* Eight rooms, breakfast served in your room, fully equipped kitchen available for guests' use. An excellent, peaceful guesthouse which enjoys good views of Table Mountain.

C Glynnville Lodge, 15 Glynnville Terrace Gardens, Centre, **T** 021-4611784, **F** 4611668. *Map 2, E7, p249* A fine restored Victorian house with a mix of double rooms, some with en suite bathroom, TV, central lounge and bar area.

C Inn with a View, 127a Kloofnek Rd, Gardens, **T** 021-4245220, **F** 4245293. *Map 2, G1, p248* Good location just before the Lower Cableway Station turn off. Comfortable double rooms with en suite bathrooms, excellent food and service, good views of Table Mountain. Highly recommended.

C Leeuwenvoet House, 93 New Church St, Tamboerskloof, **T** 021-4241133, **F** 4240495, stay@leeuwenvoet.co.za *Map 2, D4, p248* Ten rooms, comfortable homely decor, some a/c, TV, telephone, excellent breakfasts, swimming pool, off-street secure parking, close to shops and restaurants but retains a peaceful atmosphere.

C-D Metropole, 38 Long St, Centre, **T** 021-4236363, **F** 4265312. *Map 2, A8, p249* 45 double rooms, a/c, MNet TV, en suite shower and toilet. An old-fashioned town hotel with an appealing air of faded grand- eur. The better rooms are large with marble bathrooms and brass fittings, lovely old teak lift, popular café overlooking Long Street, bar, conveniently situated but a bit noisy, good value.

C-D Parker Cottage, 3 Carstens St, Tamboerskloof,
T 021-4246445, www.parkercottage.co.za *Map 2, C4, p248*
Stylish guesthouse in a restored Victorian cottage, eight en suite
bedrooms, tasteful decor, flamboyant colours with a Victorian
touch, good breakfasts, friendly service, gay-friendly.

C Table Mountain Lodge, 10A Tamboerskloof Rd, Tamboerskloof, **T** 021-4230042, **F** 4234983, tml@iafrica.com *Map 2, D4,
p248* This house was originally a lodge on a large private estate at
the foot of Table Mountain. Six spacious rooms with en suite
bathroom, TV, telephone, mature gardens and a pub for residents.

Hostels

F Ashanti Lodge, 11 Hof St, Gardens, **T** 021-4238721,
F 4238790, www.ashanti.co.za *Map 2, E6, p248* This has become
one of the city's best-known hostels, not least for its party
atmosphere. Medium size dorms and small doubles in huge old
house with polished wooden floors, large windows and communal
balconies. Some rooms surround a courtyard and small pool. Lively
bar serving good snacks, with pool table and TV MNet. Free airport
and station pickup, excellent booking centre, internet and video
room. Firmly on the busy overland truck route, can be very noisy
(and bathrooms get rather messy), but perfect for meeting people.

F The Backpack, 74 New Church St, Centre, **T** 021-4234530,
F 4230065, www.backpackers.co.za *Map 2, C5, p248* One of the
original Cape Town hostels, this has now developed into one of the
biggest and best-run. Six dorms and 10 double rooms, non-
smoking room, restaurant, lively bar, swimming pool and terrace,
games room, laundry service, reliable information, one of the most
expensive hostels, often full. Their experience shows, but there
have been reports of an "attitude problem".

F **Cat & Moose Youth Hostel**, 305 Long St, Centre, **T** 021-423 7638, **F** 4239933, catandmoose@hotmail.com *Map 2, C6, p248* Bright set-up, central location in an atmospheric old town house. Dorms and doubles are nicely furnished but a bit dark, those at front can be noisy, some have balconies overlooking Long Street, lovely courtyard with sun deck and braai, good bar, small travel centre, TV/video lounge. Laid-back, friendly atmosphere.

F **Cloudbreak Backpackers**, 219 Upper Buitenkant St, Centre, **T** 021-4616892, **F** 4611458, www.cloudbreakbackpackers.co.za *Map 2, F8, p249* Friendly and lively set-up with dorms and double rooms, internet facilities, secure parking. 15-minute stroll to the centre. We've had excellent reports of this place.

F **Elephant on Castle Backpackers**, 57 Castle St, Centre, **T/F** 021-4247524, castle@iafrica.com *Map 2, A8, p249* Small, friendly place just around the corner from the tourist office, musty dorms and doubles, only 20 beds, could do with a clean, TV lounge, free cooked dinner on Sundays, sunny balcony with braai, good place to meet people but not a place for early nights.

F **Oak Lodge**, 21 Breda St, Gardens, **T** 021-4656182, **F** 4656308, lodge@intekom.co.za *Map 2, F7, p249* Beautiful Victorian house which started out as a commune and was deve- loped into a hostel several years ago. The hippie vibe continues throughout. Large, attractive dorms, comfortable doubles (some in bungalow next door), great showers, relaxed bar, chill-out room, two video rooms and a homely kitchen. Decor is an interesting mix of African masks, ethnic fabrics and medieval wall murals.

F **Long St Backpackers**, 209 Long St, Centre, **T** 021-4230615, **F** 4231842, longstbp@mweb.co.za *Map 2, B7, p249* Lively and sociable hostel spread around leafy courtyard, small clean dorms and doubles, some with own bathrooms and balconies overlooking Long St, fully equipped kitchen, TV/video lounge, pool room, internet access, travel centre, free pickup. Good security with 24-hour police camera opposite. Lively atmosphere, occasional parties organized and weekly communal braais, but can be noisy.

F Overseas Visitors Club, 230 Long St, Centre, **T** 021-4234477, **F** 4234870, www.ovc.co.za *Map 2, C6, p248* Unlikely looking place above the Maharaja Indian restaurant, a great little hostel with only 18 beds, warm welcome from Wilmot the manager, pleasant single-sex dorms, great balcony with braai overlooking Long Street and Table Mountain, bar, excellent travel centre upstairs specializing in youth travel, one of the friendliest on Long Street.

F Zebra Crossing Backpackers, 82 New Church St, Centre, **T/F** 021-4221265, guest phone **T** 021-4239841, zebracross@ intekom.co.za *Map 2, C4, p248* Started life as a relatively small place, now expanded into house next door with more spacious rooms. Several spotless dorms plus double rooms, good views of Table Mountain, internet and travel centre, café and bar serving great breakfasts, snacks and meals, helpful management, but can be a bit too quiet.

Victoria and Alfred Waterfront

Hotels

AL Cape Grace, **T** 021-4107100, **F** 4197622, www.capegrace.com *Map 3, D11, p251* This has become one of the most luxurious hotels in Cape Town. Large development, just a short walk from the main Waterfront shops and restaurants. Very comfortable rooms with all the mod cons, traditional decor, balconies have views of the Waterfront, service and food is excellent, two bars and the Quay West restaurant, swimming pool and deck with bar.

AL Table Bay Hotel, Quay 6, Waterfront, **T** 021-4065000,
F 4180495. *Map 3, B11, p251* The latest luxury offering from the
Sun International Group, 329 rooms, all the facilities one would
expect for the price, good location with views.

A Victoria & Alfred, Pierhead, **T** 021-4196677, **F** 4198955. *Map
3, C10/11, p251* 68 luxurious and spacious a/c rooms with king-size
beds, modern furnishings, bath and separate shower, mini bar. The
rooms overlook either Table Mountain or the Piazza; the mountain
side is quieter in the evenings. Breakfast is extra but the Waterfront
Café is a perfect setting for morning treats. A smart development
with high standards in the heart of the Waterfront development.

B-D Breakwater Lodge, Portswood Rd, **T** 021-4061911,
F 4061070, www.breakwaterlodge.co.za *Map 3, C9, p251* An early
part of the Waterfront development, this hotel stands on the site of
the notorious Breakwater Prison (1859). The 330 rooms are fairly
small but comfortable. Stonebreakers restaurant, swimming pool,
ideal if you want to be close to the Waterfront. Next door is the
Graduate School of Business – many of the MBA students seem to
live in the lodge during term time.

Atlantic Seaboard

Hotels

AL-A The Bay Hotel, Victoria Rd, Camps Bay, **T** 021-4384444,
F 4384455, www.thebay.co.za *Map 5, E3, p253* 70 luxurious a/c
rooms all with views across the bay. Restaurant, swimming pool,
excellent service, a well-known place for the rich and famous.

AL Le Vendome, 20 London Rd, Sea Point, **T** 021-4301200,
F 4301500, www.le-vendome.co.za *Map 4, B5, p252* A large,

well-designed luxury hotel. All rooms a/c, satellite TV, internet facilities, private fax, room safe, two restaurants, swimming pool, secure parking.

AL Peninsula, 313 Beach Rd, Sea Point, **T** 021-4398888, **F** 4398886, www.peninsula.co.za *Map 4, E2, p252* 'Timeshare Hotel' with 110 suites including kitchen facilities. Friendly service, bar, restaurant and swimming pool. Perfect location right on one of the few sandy stretches of seafront, a short walk from all the shops and restaurants in Sea Point. The rooms in the newer part are better.

A-B The Clarendon, 67 Kloof Rd, Sea Point, **T** 021-4393224, **F** 4346855, www.clarendon.co.za *Map 4, F3, p252* Pleasant guesthouse with seven spacious rooms, some with mountain views, all with en suite bathroom, TV and safe. Peaceful location and only a short walk to the shops in Sea Point, secure parking.

B-C Blackheath Lodge, 6 Blackheath Rd, Sea Point, **T** 021-4392541, **F** 4399776, www.blackheathlodge.co.za *Map 3, D2, p250* Five smart double rooms in a converted Victorian mansion. Off-street parking, TV, mini bar, palm-fringed patio, swimming pool, but no children under 14. Recommended for couples.

B Cape Victoria, 13 Torbay Rd, Green Point, **T/F** 021-4397721. *Map 3, D6, p250* A mix of exclusive hotel service and the privacy of a guesthouse, 10 tastefully furnished rooms with antiques, en suite bathrooms, TV, mini bar and views of the sea or Table Mountain, swimming pool, booking essential.

B The Glen Guest House, 3 Glen Rd, Sea Point, **T** 021-4390072. *Map 4, C5, p252* Italian-style villa with views of Signal Hill and tropical garden with palm trees and shaded seating areas. 11 rooms, each decorated with fine pieces of furniture and art, TV, bar, fridge, telephone, swimming pool, restaurant.

B-C t'Huijs Haerlem, 25 Main Drive, Sea Point, **T** 021-4346434, **F** 4392506. *Map 3, E3, p250* Five rooms with en suite facilities, friendly relaxed atmosphere, comfortable and homely furnishings, magnificent views towards the Atlantic, solar-heated salt-water swimming pool, good value.

B Monkey Valley, Mountain Rd, Noordhoek, **T** 021-7891391, **F** 7891143. *Map 1, F2, p246* Luxurious self-catering thatched log cottages set in woodland overlooking Noordhoek Bay. Each has a secluded veranda with superb views.

B-C Winchester Mansions, 221 Beach Rd, Sea Point, **T** 021-4342351, **F** 4340215, www.winchester.co.za *Map 4, A6, p252* A well-run family hotel that has managed to retain plenty of old charm despite its size. 35 stylish double rooms, each with TV, en suite bathroom, and 18 suites. All rooms overlook a large, tranquil courtyard where meals are served beneath the palms. *Harvey's*, a new sea-facing restaurant, offers innovative meals.

C Bay Atlantic, 3 Berkley Rd, Camps Bay, **T** 021-4384341, **T** 0827778007 (mob). *Map 5, D4, p253* A few rooms in a luxury villa, plus a beachside villa only 150 m from the sea. All rooms with TV, set in mature gardens with swimming pool. Evening meals available. Book well in advance during the peak season.

C Brenwin & Chamel Guest House, 1 Thornhill Rd, Green Point, **T** 021-4340220, **F** 4393465, brenwin@netactive.co.za *Map 3, D7, p251* 14 large rooms with en suite bathrooms, shady patio overlooking tidy tropical garden with swimming pool, within easy walking distance of the Waterfront. Very helpful owner who enjoys helping and advising guests with their travel plans.

C Whale Cottage Guesthouse, 57 Camps Bay Drive, Camps Bay, **T** 021-4383840, **F** 4384388, www.whalecottage.com *Map 5,*

H9, p253 Four double rooms with en suite bathrooms, small tasteful place with marine decor, breakfast deck overlooking the beach, good views of the Twelve Apostles, satellite TV and internet.

D Bellevue Manor House, 5 Bellevue Rd, Sea Point, **T** 021-4340375, **F** 4391511, www.bellevue.co.za *Map 4, C6, p252* Nine rooms in beautiful Victorian town house with stylish iron balconies and fine palm trees, all rooms have en suite bathrooms, TV, non smoking, laundry, friendly service.

D Kinneret Guest House, 11 Arthur's Rd, **T** 021-4399237, Sea Point, **F** 4348998. *Map 4, D5, p252* Ten light and airy rooms, private bathroom, fridge, TV, telephone. A comfortable, lemon yellow two-storey house with first floor balcony, short walk from sea and shops.

Hostels

E-F Carnaby Backpacker, 219 Main Rd, Three Anchor Bay, Sea Point, **T** 021-4397410, **F** 4391222, www.carnabybackpacker.co.za *Map 3, D3, p250* Building used to be a hotel, now offers great value double rooms with en suite facilities, as well as spacious dorms, and all the usual facilities expected in a well managed backpacker hostel. Bar, swimming pool, travel service. In the Top-10 hostels.

F Brown Sugar, 1 Main Rd, Green Point, **T** 021-4330413, **F** 0860102291, www.brownsugar.get.to *Map 3, E9, p251* Busy but laid-back hostel near the Waterfront, on noisy Main Road, dorms, doubles and some camping space, shared bathrooms, popular bar with party atmosphere, Ganeshi restaurant with chill-out Goa lounge, good place to meet people.

F St John's Waterfront Lodge, 6 Braemar Rd, Green Point, **T** 021-4391404, **F** 4391424, www.stjohns.co.za *Map 3, E8, p251* Closest hostel to the Waterfront. Dorms and doubles spread across two houses, sundeck, two pools, bar, braai, friendly and helpful staff, travel centre.

F Globe Trotter, 17 Queens Rd, Sea Point, **T** 021-4341539, guest phone **T** 021-4397113. *Map 4, F2, p252* Small town house on the fringe of Sea Point with three dorms, TV lounge, dining area, secure lockers. An easy walk along the coast to Clifton beach and Bantry Bay, public transport to city centre, cheapest in town.

F Stans Halt Youth Hostel, The Glen, Camps Bay , **T** 021-4389037. *Map 1, C2, p246* A great, cheap alternative amongst the super-wealthy on the slopes of Table Mountain. Five dorms with six beds in each, set in a wooded garden, with kitchen, breakfasts and dinner to order. Bike hire, very popular in season, call in advance.

F Sunflower Stop, 179 Main Rd, Sea Point, **T** 021-4346535, **F** 4346501, www.sunflowerstop.co.za *Map 4, E4, p252* Dorms with more room than most, doubles, excellent clean place with a huge kitchen, meals available too. Swimming pool, bar, satellite TV, tours and travel advice. Great location. Free airport and city pickup.

Southern Suburbs

Hotels

AL The Cellars-Hohenhort, 93 Brommersulei Rd, Constantia, **T** 021-7942137, **F** 7942149. *15 mins from Cape Town city centre. Map 1, D3, p246* Luxury hotel in two converted manor houses and a wine estate, with 15 spacious suites and 38 individually decorated rooms. Thoughtfully renovated, two excellent restaurants, one has a good reputation for French and English meals, the other for Cape Malay dishes. Two swimming pools, tennis court, set in nine acres of mature gardens overlooking False Bay.

AL-A Constantia Uitsig, Spaanschemat, River Rd, Constantia, **T** 021-7946500, **F** 7947605. *Map 1, D3, p246* Spacious, cool cottages set in neat gardens with views across vineyards to the mountains, short drive to the city centre. Two restaurants, one by the swimming pool. The food is excellent. Reserve in advance.

A Alphen Hotel, Alphen Dr, **T** 021-7945011, **F** 7945710. *20-mins' drive from the city centre, located at the head of Constantia Valley.* *Map 1, D3, p246* 26 spacious rooms in one of the most elegant 18th-century Cape Dutch estates. Suites and rooms are decorated with fine antiques, beautiful rugs on polished floors, and log fires during winter months. Lunches are served in a pub or in the gardens during the summer, and in the evening there is a popular restaurant in the Manor House which attracts many non-residents. Swimming pool and free use of a nearby sports centre.

AL-A Steenberg Country Hotel, 20 km from Cape Town in the Constantia Valley, **T** 021-7132222, **F** 7132221, www.steenberg hotel.com *Map 1, D3, p246* Luxurious country hotel with tasteful rooms, some in converted farm buildings. Swimming pool, horse riding and golf all available to guests. Relaxed and friendly.

A The Vineyard Hotel, Protea Rd, Newlands, **T** 021-6833044, **F** 6833365. *Map 1, C4, p246* 155 a/c rooms in an 18th-century house; the decor is early Cape Dutch with yellow-wood furniture. Coffee shop and pâtisserie, elegant restaurant, swimming pool and old gardens. One of the best value upmarket hotels in Cape Town.

B Harfield Cottage, 26 1st Avenue, Claremont, **T** 021-6837376, **F** 6716715, harfield@grm.co.za *Map 1, C4, p246* A comfortable, smart B&B, spacious, en suite rooms with TV, mini bar and views of Table Mountain. Lounge/bar, sundeck and swimming pool, bicycle hire, secure off-street parking. Relaxing ambience during the winter months when log fires help to keep you warm.

C Devonshire House, 6 Lovers Walk, Rondebosch,
T/F 021-6861519. *Map 1, C4, p246* Homely restored house with
five double rooms, all with en suite bathroom, TV, friendly service.
The old wooden floors greatly add to the atmosphere.

Hostels

F The Green Elephant, 57 Milton Rd, Observatory,
T 0800-222722/4486539, guest telephone **T** 021-4475842,
greenelephant@iafrica.com *Map 7, A2, p255* A full-on backpacker
joint, not to everyone's taste but helpful and knowledgeable staff,
plenty going on in the area away from the city centre, old house
hidden behind high walls in compact suburb, dorms plus a couple
of double rooms with four-poster beds, happy to organize trips to
the regional sights, free collection, have a second house with five
double rooms which is very popular.

F SA's The Alternative Place, 64 St Michaels Rd, Claremont,
T/F 021-6742396, alternative_place@mweb.co.za *Map 1, C4,
p246* Clean dorms sleeping four, two double rooms, kitchen,
garden with pool, bar and braai. A small homely setup run by
Susan and Alun who have excellent Southern and East African
travel experience. A bit far from the town centre, but worth
checking out. Free airport pickup.

False Bay

Hotels

A Quayside Hotel, Quayside Centre, Wharf St, Simon's Town,
T 021-7863838, **F** 7862241, www.quayside.co.za *Map 1, I3,
p247* Situated on the seafront in the centre of town. 28 double
rooms, all with nice views across the harbour. A smart

development in a great location, but rather over-priced. Book well in advance for visits during local holidays.

B-C British Hotel Apartments, 90 St George's St, Simon's Town, **T/F** 021-7904930, **T** 082-5585689 (mob). *Map 1, I3, p247* Four elegant self-catering apartments in a fully restored Victorian building. Three bedrooms in each, sleeping up to six, smart polished wooden floors, sea views from the magnificent balconies, breakfasts available on request. Highly recommended.

B-C Tudor House by the Sea, 43 Simon's Town Rd, **T** 021-7826238, **F** 7825027. *Map 1, I3, p247* Six luxury self-catering apartments, all mod cons, serviced daily, secure parking, secluded gardens, ideal for a longer break for those wishing to explore the area and not be confined to a hotel, very popular in season, advance reservations necessary.

C Boulders Beach Guest House, 4 Boulders Place, **T** 021-7861758, **F** 7861825, www.bouldersbeach.co.za *Map 1, I3, p247* This friendly, well-run guesthouse is a firm favourite with us. 18 double rooms with en suite bathrooms, most arranged around a paved yard (without sea view), simple refreshing design, just metres from the beach. At night you're likely to see penguins exploring the grounds after everyone has gone home.

C The Lamp Guesthouse, 14 Watson Rd, Muizenberg, **T** 021-7881041, **F** 7881070. *Map 1, F4, p246* Very comfortable rooms (one is decorated to look like a safari tent), superb breakfasts, small veranda and garden, no smoking.

D Glenview Cottage, 56 Camilla St, Glencairn Heights, **T** 021-7821324. *Map 1, H3, p247* Family-run B&B, two double rooms, en suite bathroom, TV, small fridge, private patio, secure off-street parking, separate entrance, braai facilities in the garden.

Hostels

E-F Top Sail House, 176 St George's St, Simon's Town,
T 021-7865537. *Map 1, I3, p247* Backpacker's hostel set in an old
convent school building, quiet place with dorms, doubles, balcony
overlooking St George's Street, bike hire, friendly.

E-F Wipeout Backpackers, corner Camp and Main Rd,
Muizenberg, **T** 021-7884803, **F** 7883700, wipeout@iafrica.com
Map 1, F4, p246 Relaxed place on busy Main Rd, popular with
surfers, TV MNet, bar, free use of mountain bikes and surf boards.

F Harbour Side Backpackers, 136 Main Rd, Kalk Bay,
T 021-7882943, **F** 7886452, harboursidebackpackers@hotmail.com
Map 1, G3, p247 Hostel above a pub, eight-bed dorms, double
beds with views across False Bay, good value restaurant serving
excellent wholesome meals, plenty of trips and sporting adventures
organized, close to *The Brass Bell*, good alternative to Cape Town.

The Winelands

Stellenbosch

AL Lanzerac Manor, Jonkershoek Rd, **T** 021-8871132,
F 8872310, www.lanzerac.co.za *Map 8, E2/3, p256* 48 rooms,
some around a patio and swimming pool, spacious and well
equipped, three restaurants. A smart hotel based around a luxury
18th- century Dutch manor house. The food in the main dining
room does not measure up to the status of the hotel, but the *Vinkel
en Koljander* restaurant serves excellent food, closed in the evenings.

AL d'Ouwe Werf, 30 Church St, **T** 021-8871608, **F** 8874626,
www.ouwewerf.com *Map 8, E2/3, p256* Converted Georgian house

with 25 a/c rooms, antique furnishings, polished floors, off-street parking, pool, celebrating its 200th year, vine-shaded terrace.

B De Goue Druif, 110 Dorp St, **T** 021-8833555, **F** 8833588, www.gouedruif.hypemart.net *Map 8, E2/3, p256* Ultra smart and modern guesthouse, luxury bedrooms, lush garden, gym, sauna and steambath. Ideal location for exploring town on foot.

B Dorpshuis, 22 Dorp St, **T** 021-8839881, **F** 8839884, www.relaishotels.co.za *Map 8, E2/3, p256* 15 a/c rooms, marble-clad bathrooms, TV, private patio, antiques adorn each room, neat gardens, swimming pool, smart Victorian town house.

B Stellenbosch, 162 Dorp St, **T** 021-8873644, **F** 8873673, stb-hotel@mweb.co.za *Map 8, E2/3, p256* 20 a/c rooms in a gorgeous building which is protected as a National Monument. Seafood restaurant, brasserie and bar. Smart option in the centre.

B-C L'Auberge Rozendal, Omega St, Rozendal Farm, **T** 021-8838737, **F** 8838738. *Map 8, E2/3, p256* Family-run guesthouse with 16 double rooms, small dining room, pleasant veranda over-looking woods. Swimming pool, shady gardens, a fine old house.

C Wilfra Court, 16 Hine St, **T/F** 021-8896091, **T** 082-9200085 (mob). *5 km from the centre, off the R44 road to Paarl. Map 8, p256* Two double rooms with shared bathroom breakfast included, run by William and Francis. Anyone with an interest in South African political affairs should stay here. This was the first guesthouse in the region run by coloured people and William was an MP for more than 30 years. Strongly recommended. A unique experience.

F Stumble Inn, 12 Market St, **T/F** 021-8874049, stumble@iafri ca.com *Map 8, E2/3, p256* Popular hostel in two separate old Cape houses. Spacious double rooms and cramped dorms. Original house

Sleeping

has attractive garden, bar, TV room, kitchen, hammocks; other house has a small pool. Relaxed. By far the best budget option.

Franschhoek

AL-A Auberge du Quartier Français, corner of Wilhelmina and Berg St, **T** 021-8762151, **F** 8763105, res@lqf.co.za *Map 8, E6, p256* An elegant country house with 14 large en suite rooms all with fireplaces and pleasant views over the gardens. Small central swimming pool and peaceful courtyard. The attached restaurant is rated as one of the best in the Western Cape, but the food can be fussy and disappointing. Nevertheless, a good hotel for a treat.

B Auberge La Dauphine, PO Box 384, **T/F** 021-8762606, moates@ct.lia.net *Map 8, E6, p256* One of the most peaceful locations in the valley. Five luxury rooms each with a spacious lounge in a carefully restored and converted wine cellar. The house is surrounded by beautiful gardens and vineyards. Large swimming pool, guided tours of the farm, plus mountain bike trails and horse-riding in the nearby mountains. Recommended.

B La Cabriere, Middagkrans Rd, **T** 021-8764780, lacabriere@icon. co.za *Map 8, F6, p256* Small luxurious guesthouse, four a/c en suite rooms with Provençal decor, fireplaces and views of vineyards and mountains. Understated and stylish spot, great location.

B Franschhoek Country House, Main Rd, **T** 021-8763386, www.fch.co.za *Map 8, E6, p256* Smart, restored country house with six neat and spacious rooms, four-poster beds, excellent service, mature gardens, swimming pool.

B-C Résidence Klein Oliphants Hoek, 14 Akademie St, **T/F** 021-8762566, www.kleinoliphantshoek.com *Map 8, E6, p256* A very fine guesthouse in the centre of the village. Six cosy and comfortable a/c double rooms, en suite bathrooms and MNet TV. Lounge, library, swimming pool. Recommended.

C Le Jardinet, 3 Klein Cabriere St, **T/F** 8762186, regeorge@ mweb.co.za *Map 8, E6, p256* A peaceful B&B situated in a quiet side street just a few minutes' walk from the restaurants and shops. Double rooms with en suite bathroom, each overlooking the garden. A favourite in the village. Excellent value. Recommended.

D-F La Bri Holiday Farm, Robertsvlei Rd, **T** 021-8763133. *Map 8, p256* Choice of self-catering cottages which can sleep up to six, or dormitory, peaceful rural location, swim in the farm dam, must have your own transport to get here.

Paarl

AL Grande Roche, Plantasie St, **T** 021-8632727, **F** 8632220, www.granderoche.com *Map 8, B4, p256* An 18th-century manor which has quickly established itself as one of the top hotels in South Africa. A collection of restored farm buildings stand in peaceful gardens, surrounded by vineyards. 35 luxury a/c suites, non-smoking rooms, tennis courts, swimming pool, gym. *Bosman's* restaurant is regarded as one of the best in the Cape – the crystal chandeliers say it all. Will collect from Cape Town airport.

AL-A Zomerlust, 193 Main St, **T** 021-8722117, **F** 8728312, www.zomerlust.co.za *Map 8, B4, p256* 14 rooms in a restored country house in the centre of town. Some rooms are in converted stables. Courtyard, terrace, cellar pub and popular attached restaurant – *Kontreihuis*, check for winter discounts, swimming pool.

B Lemoenkloof Guest House, 396a Main St, **T** 021-8723782, **F** 8727532. *Map 8, B4, p256* Luxurious country house with plenty of character and atmosphere. 14 a/c rooms with TV and mini bar.

Shady gardens, healthy large breakfasts, evening meals on request, swimming pool.

B Palmiet Valley, **T** 021-8627741, **F** 8626891, www.palmiet.co.za *Map 8, B4, p256* A restored historic homestead, located on an estate to the east of the town centre. Six spacious double rooms with en suite bathrooms, satellite TV in each room, room safes, each decorated with antiques, neat garden, swimming pool.

B Roggeland Country House, Roggeland Rd, Dal Josafat, **T** 021-8682501, **F** 8682113, rog@iafrica.com *Map 8, B4, p256* A wonderful Cape Dutch farmhouse with 11 luxury rooms, with en suite bathroom, mature gardens, swimming pool, excellent cuisine.

C Goedemoed Country Inn, Cecilia St, **T** 021-8631102, wsteenkamp@hixnet.co.za *Map 8, B4, p256* A fine Cape Dutch family home, relaxed atmosphere, nine en suite rooms, swimming pool, set in the middle of a wine estate, good value.

D-E Amberg Guest Farm, Klein Drakenstein, **T** 021-8630982, amberg@mweb.co.za *Map 8, B4, p256* One of the few budget options in the area, great setting with mountain views, mix of cottages and dorm accommodation, self-catering or B&B, large pool, indigenous garden, braai.

The Whale Coast

Hermanus

A The Marine, Marine Drive, **T** 028-3131000, **F** 3130160, www.marine-hermanus.co.za Large, luxurious hotel dominating the Waterfront – the best hotel in town. Stylish decor, great views, heated swimming pool, jacuzzi, billiard room, art gallery, average restaurant.

B Auberge Burgundy, 16 Harbour Rd, **T** 028-3131201, **F** 3131204. 14 rooms, luxury doubles and suites, the penthouse can sleep six, all set in an immaculate garden full of herbs and mature trees. Has a luxurious inner courtyard plus a swimming pool with a fine view across Walker Bay. Recommended.

B Windsor Hotel, 49 Marine Drive, **T** 028-3123727, **F** 3122181, www.windsor-hotel.com Large and popular hotel set on cliffs overlooking the ocean. En suite rooms with TV. Excellent views from the glassed-in lounge. Slightly plain restaurant.

C Kenjockity, 15 Church St, **T** 028-3121772. A typical old Hermanus house which started life as a boarding house in the 1920s. Thoughtfully restored with 11 rooms, some with en suite bathroom, friendly and helpful owners, small breakfasts, within walking distance of the bay and shops.

D-F Zoete Inval, 23 Main Rd, **T/F** 028-3121242. Seven double rooms, TV lounge, small library, kitchen facilities available, bicycle hire, laundry service, secure parking. Dorm beds available for backpackers, will meet the Baz Bus at *Bot River Hotel*.

F Moby's Backpackers, 8 Main Rd, **T** 028-3132361, **F** 3123519, www.mobys.co.za Great backpackers offering a good range of rooms: doubles, dorms sleeping six to eight, family rooms, all en suite. Two bars, one for residents only, large garden with pool, daily braais, internet, TV lounge, fully- equipped kitchen. Friendly and laid-back place, do Baz Bus pickups. Also organize very cheap shark dives and the usual excursions.

Unlike the rest of South Africa, Cape Town likes to eat out, a fact which is reflected in its multitude of restaurants – and the extent to which they get packed out. The city is blessed with spectacular outdoor eating locations, as well as fresh ingredients and first-rate cooking. Summer is the most popular time for eating out, and the Waterfront, perhaps the city's most popular eating area, gets very busy. Booking ahead is often a good idea and essential on Saturday nights.

You are likely to eat very well here. Much of the food is seafood, which is always good value and usually very fresh. Meat lovers are very well served – South Africans are big meat eaters, and it tends to be of high quality, especially steak. Exotic game such as kudu or springbok also makes it onto plenty of menus. Vegetarians, however, may have a harder time. Although Cape Town is more sympathetic to non-meat dishes than most of the country, choices are limited and often quite bland. There is a handful of vegetarian restaurants though, and these are generally very good.

R **Eating codes**

Price

RRR R200 and over
RR R50-199
R R49 and under
Price of a meal for one with wine

Cape Town offers a full range of international restaurants, from French bistros and sushi bars to Moçambique seafood. Its most unique cuisine is Cape Malay cooking, an interesting blend of fiery curries softened with coconut milk or preserved fruits. Although there are surprisingly few Cape Malay restaurants, some of the more popular dishes such as bobotie, a sweet-spicy dish of minced beef topped with egg custard, is served in plenty of restaurants. A local term to listen out for is braai, quite simply cooking food on a barbecue, usually accompanied by copious quantities of alcohol. Braais are incredibly popular and in summer are a major form of entertainment for Capetonians. The staple diet for most South Africans is stiff maize porridge, known as pap, and served with a stew. It is not a dish that tourists are likely to encounter, unless they are invited into an African home, although there are a couple of 'traditional' African restaurants in town which serve pap and game.

The city centre

Restaurants

RRR Aubergine, 39 Barnet St, Gardens, **T** 021-4654909. *Evenings only, Mon-Sat. Map 2, D8, p249* Sophisticated and award-winning menu, modern slants on classical European dishes, excellent wine list. One of the best in town. Stylish shaded court-yard, lounge/bar, good service. Recommended.

★ **Al fresco restaurants**

Best

- •Kirstenbosch Restaurant, p150
- •Quay Four, V & A Waterfront, p168
- •Black Marlin, Miller's Point, p152
- •The Brass Bell, Kalk Bay, p154
- •Table Mountain caféteria, p140

RRR Blue Danube, 102 New Church St, Tamboerskloof,
T 021-4233624. *Closed Sun and Mon lunch. Map 2, C4, p248*
Chef Thomas Sinn combines traditional Austrian dishes with an
international fusion menu, served in a fine old building with
spacious rooms and mountain views.

RRR Cape Colony, Mount Nelson Hotel, 76 Orange St, Centre,
T 021-4831000. *1830-2230. Map 2, D5, p248* One of Cape Town's
finest restaurants in the impressive setting of the Mount Nelson.
Dishes are classical Cape Cuisine plus a couple of Thai and African
dishes. Impeccable service.

RRR Five Flies, 14 Keerom St, Centre, **T** 021-4231048. *1100-2300.*
Map 2, B7, p249 Preferred haunt of lawyers and judges, attractive
restaurant and old-fashioned bar, high ceilings, starched tablecloths.

RRR Kotobuki, 3 Mill St, Gardens, **T** 021-4623675. *1100-2300
closed Mon. Map 2, E6, p248* Japanese, no-frills top-class menu,
expensive for Cape Town, but a favourite amongst the Japanese
community.

RR The Africa Café, Heritage Sq, 108 Short Market St, Centre,
T 021-4220221. *Mon-Sat 1800-2300. Map 3, H10, p251* The
original in Observatory moved here recently, but despite becoming
more upmarket, the food remains an excellent introduction to the

continent's cuisines. The menu is a set 'feast' and includes 10 dishes that rove around the continent, from Malawian Mbatata balls and Kenyan patties, to Cape Malay mango chicken curry and Egyptian dips. The price includes the chance to order more of the dishes you like, as well as coffee and dessert. Good value and excellent service, although very touristy.

RR Biesmiellah, 2 Upper Wale St, Centre, **T** 021-4230850. *Mon-Sat, lunch and dinner. Map 2, A6, p248* One of the better known and well-established Malay restaurants, serving a delicious Indian and Cape Malay dishes. If you like your curry hot then this is the place to come, a real treat for any fan of spicy food. No alcohol.

RR Café Paradiso, 110 Kloof St, Gardens, **T** 021 4238653. *0900/1000-2300. Map 2, F3, p248* Tuscan setting for this relaxed Italian restaurant. Some fine local dishes, but the best options are the Italian dishes. Recommended.

RR Rozenhof, 18 Kloof St, Gardens, **T** 021-4241968. *Mon-Fri 1230-2300, Sat 1900-late. Map 2, C5, p248* Smart restaurant set in an attractive 18th-century town house, decorated with local art work and chandeliers, food to match the surrounds, sensible light dishes full of flavour, look out for seasonal dishes such as aspara gus and salads, good choice for vegetarians.

RR Mama Africa, 178 Long St, **T** 021-4248634. *1900-late. Map 2, B7, p249* Popular restaurant and bar serving 'traditional' African dishes often with great live music. Popular with tourists, tasty food if overpriced, excellent service. Centrepiece is a bright green carved mamba-shaped bar. Slightly tacky but a very fun place.

RR Pagoda Inn, 29 Bree St, Centre, **T** 021-4252033. *Map 3, G11, 251* Chinese restaurant with a good selection of dishes, choice of small or large portions.

RR Saigon, corner Camp and Kloof sts, Gardens, **T** 021-4247670, zenasia@iafrica.com *1200-1500, 1800-2300.* *Map 2, E4, p248* Superb Vietnamese cuisine, very popular place overlooking busy Kloof St, brilliant crystal spring rolls, barbecued duck and caramelized pork with black pepper. Book ahead. Recommended.

RR Star*, 273 Long St, **T** 021-4246576. *1100-late.* *Map 2, B6, p248* Trendy establishment serving good seafood, salads and a couple of Portuguese dishes. Friendly service and getting popular with a well-heeled young crowd. Turns into a fiercely fashionable bar from about 2300. Only seven tables, so come early or book.

RR Sukhothai, 12 Mill St, Centre, **T** 021-4655846. *Map 2, C6, p248* Good Thai cuisine, set menus for the confused, advisable to book at the weekend, authentically Thai, hot and spicy.

RR Yindee's, 22 Camp St, Tamboerskloof, **T** 021-4221012. *Mon-Fri 1200-late, Sat and Sun 1800-late.* *Map 2, E4, p248* An excellent Thai restaurant serving authentic spicy curries and soups. Served in a sprawling Victorian house with traditional low tables. Service can be very slow, but the place is always popular, so book ahead.

RR yum, 2 Deer Park Dr, Vredehoek, **T** 021-4617607. *1000-2300.* *Map 2, H8, p249* Stylish deli and restaurant serving excellent sandwiches, salads and original pasta dishes, such as roast lamb tortellini or goat's cheese and roasted pepper lasagne. Good service, relaxed young crowd, delicious pickles and chutneys on sale. Recommended.

R Arnold's, 60 Kloof St, Gardens, **T** 021-4244344, www.arnolds. co.za *1200-late.* *Map 2, D4, p248* Good value lunch spot on busy Kloof Street, good salads, pasta and more substantial meals like ostrich steak. Fast, friendly service.

R **The Crypt**, 1 Wale St, below St George's Cathedral, **T** 021-4249426. *1000-1600. Map 2, B8, p249* Despite its suspect location, this restaurant has lovely sunny tables set out on Wale Street and serves the usual sandwiches and salads plus excellent daily pasta specials. Perfect for people-watching in the summer, or huddling in the vaulted interior in winter.

R **Maeströs**, Kloof St, Gardens, **T** 021-4243015. *1000-late. Map 2, D4, p248* Restaurant and pub, food of a high standard.

R **Marco's African Place**, 15 Rose St, Centre, **T** 021-4235412. *1800-2300. Map 3, H10, p251* African menu, live music, huge, smoky place with a friendly atmosphere, excellent starters but main courses are disappointing.

R **Ocean Basket**, 75 Kloof St, Gardens, **T** 021-4220322. *0900-2300, open weekends in the evening. Map 2, D5, p248* A successful, good value franchise serving seafood and salads, pleasant setting with a large courtyard at the back. No bookings, expect to queue outside on the street.

R **Primi Piatti**, Greenmarket Sq, Centre, **T** 021-4247466. *Mon-Sat 0900-late. Map 2, A8, p249* Lively spot for lunch overlooking the square from the huge open windows. Superb pizzas, good pasta and salads, huge portions at reasonable prices, popular with a young fashionable crowd.

R **Shambhala**, 134 Long St, Centre, **T** 021-4265452, www.shambhala.co.za *0900-2100. Map 2, A7, p249* Relaxed vegetarian restaurant serving salads, sandwiches and good daily specials. Calm Buddhism-inspired decor, friendly service, great spot for lunch.

★ **Cafés**

Best
- Mr Pickwicks, Long Street, p140
- Olympia Café, Kalk Bay, p155
- Charly's Bakery, Roeland Street, p140
- Obz Café, Observatory, p151
- New York Bagels, Sea Point, p148

Cafés

R Charly's Bakery, 20 Roeland St, Centre, **T** 021-4615181. *0800-1600. Map 2, C8, p249* Tiny café serving brilliant cakes, pastries and pies – don't miss the spinach and feta pie.

R Mr Pickwicks, 158 Long St, Centre. *0900-very late. Map 2, B6, p248* Trendy spot serving the best milkshakes in town, excellent French loaf sandwiches, healthy salads, large pasta portions, licensed, gets very busy with an after-work crowd, open late. Also sells tickets to Cape Town's major club nights and gigs.

R Naked on Kloof, 47 Kloof St, Gardens, **T** 021-4244748. *1000-late. Map 2, C5, p248* Healthy fast-food joint selling wraps, sandwiches and juices, open late so good for a mid-Saturday night snack.

R Sunflower Health Café, 161 Longmarket St, Centre. *0800-1600. Map 2, B7, p249* Good value vegetarian meals, plus shop.

R Table Mountain Cafeteria, Table Mountain, **T** 021-4248181, www.tablemountain.co.za Overpriced and hectic cafeteria, but in one of the best locations in town. Self-service sandwiches, cold drinks, ice creams and hot meals. Also sells beers that you can take outside to watch sunset.

R **Yellow Pepper Deli**, 138 Long St, Centre. *Mon-Sat 0800-2300. Map 2, A1, p249* Good breakfast, exciting and unusual range of home-cooked European dishes, trendy and very popular.

Victoria and Alfred Waterfront

Restaurants

RRR **Baia**, top floor, Victoria Wharf, **T** 021-4210935. *1200-1500, 1900-2300. Map 3, B11, p251* Newest addition to Cape Town's fine restaurants. Very smart (and expensive) venue specialising in seafood. Delicious, rich dishes following a Moçambique theme – try the beer-baked prawns. Stylish, moodily lit interior with views of Table Mountain, slightly erratic service. Book ahead.

RRR **Emily's**, Clock Tower centre, **T** 021-4211133. *1200-1430, 1830-late. Map 3, C10, p251* The old Woodstock favourite recently moved to the top floor of the new Clock Tower centre. Very smart restaurant serving excellent French-style cuisine, great views from balcony overlooking the Waterfront, polite service, popular, book.

RR **Aldos**, ground floor, Victoria Wharf, **T** 021-4217846. *Mon-Sat 1200-1400, 1800-late. Map 3, B11, p251* One of the better Italian restaurants in town, reflected in the imaginative range of dishes on offer.

RR **Arlindos**, ground floor, Victoria Wharf. *Map 3, B11, p251* Mouth-watering selection of game and seafood dishes, excellent calamari, reasonable wines, polite and attentive service, outside terrace gets a bit crowded. Recommended.

RR **Cape Town Fish Market**, ground floor, Victoria Wharf, **T** 021-4135977. *1200-2300. Map 3, B11, p251* Popular fish restaurant, but the reason to come here is the revolving sushi bar, serving excellent sushi and sashimi. Dishes on offer are limited but very fresh and good value.

RR Cantina Tequila, Quay 5, Victoria Wharf, **T** 021-4190207. *1000-late. Map 3, B11, p251* Full range of Mexican dishes, good cocktails, live music Wednesday-Sunday, outside terrace, touristy, indifferent service and erratic food.

RR Den Anker, Pierhead, **T** 021-4190249. *1100-2300. Map 3, C10, p251* Popular Belgian (Flemish) restaurant and bar, continental feel, high ceiling flying the various duchy flags, newspaper plastered pillars, airy leafy bar, views across Alfred Basin of Table Mountain, civilized atmosphere. Plenty of Belgian dishes to sample plus an amazing selection of imported bottle beers.

RR The Edge, Pierhead, **T** 021-4212583. *1200-late. Map 3, C10, p251* Terrace tables on a first-come basis, spicy mix of Cape cuisine with an emphasis on seafood dishes, a good mix of South African meals.

RR Hildebrand, Pierhead, **T** 021-4253385. *1100-2300. Map 3, C10, p251* Well-established Italian seafood place, excellent pasta, good reputation, touristy given the location.

RR Mortons on the Wharf, upstairs, Victoria Wharf, **T** 021-4183633. *1200-1500, 1800-late. Map 3, B11, p251* A busy New Orleans-style restaurant and bar, Creole fish dishes or spicy Cajun country food, a playful and fun evening with live music, Jazz, Mardi Gras and Blues, check out the Sunday Jazz brunch.

RR The Musselcracker, Victoria Wharf, **T** 021-4194300. *1200-2200. Map 3, B11, p251* Popular seafood restaurant and oyster bar, lunchtime seafood buffets, some bad reports but remains busy.

R **Quay Four**, T 021-4192008. *1100-late. Map 3, B11, p251*
Pleasant bar-restaurant set on a shady deck overlooking the
harbour. Very popular for seafood lunches served in individual
frying pans, and a good spot for drinks at sundown or an
evening meal.

Cafés

R **Charters Coffee Shop**, Pierhead, T 021-4193103.
0900-1700. Map 3, B11, p251 In the restored grey and white Old
Port Captain's Building, also home to Waterfront Charters Boat
Trips, sandwiches and light lunches.

R **Mugg & Bean**, Victoria Wharf, T 021-4196451. *0900-1700.
Map 3, B11, p251* Also branch in Cavendish Sq, Claremont, and the
Lifestyles centre on Kloof St. Café serving mouth-watering muffins,
cakes and sandwiches and good coffee.

Atlantic Seaboard

Restaurants

RRR **Buena Vista Social Café**, Main Rd, Green Point, T 021-
4330611. *1200-late. Map 3, D8, p251* Cuban-themed bar and
restaurant. Great decor, trendy Cuban photography, plush chairs to
lounge in or breezy balcony overlooking Main Rd. Live Latin music
at weekends, very fashionable, excellent but pricey food.

RRR **Mr Chan**, 178a Main Rd, Sea Point, T 021-4392239.
1200-1500, 1800-2200. Map 4, C5, p252 Smart upmarket restaurant serving Pekingese, Cantonese and Szechuan meals. Expensive
but some top-quality dishes. Recommended for a treat.

Best

★ **Seafood restaurants**
- The Codfather, Camps Bay, p144
- Bertha's, Simon's Town, p152
- Blues, Camps Bay, p144
- Baia, V & A Waterfront, p141
- Fish on the Rocks, Hout Bay, p146

RRR Blues, Victoria Rd, Camps Bay, **T** 021-4382040. *1200-2200. Map 5, E3, p253* Popular and well-known seafood place with superb views, Californian-style menu served to a beautiful crowd. Good, stylish food, although you pay for the restaurant's reputation.

RRR The Codfather, corner Geneva Drive and The Drive, Camps Bay, **T** 021-4380782. *1200-1600, 1900-2300. Map 5, F3, p253* One of the best seafood restaurants in Cape Town, stylish laid-back place offering a range of superbly fresh seafood. No menu – the waiter takes you to a counter and you pick and choose whatever you like the look of. Also has an excellent sushi bar. Highly recommended.

RRR The Restaurant, 51a Somerset Rd, Green Point, **T** 021-4192921. *Mon-Sat 1800-2300. Map 3, E8, p251* One of Cape Town's finest, serving superb seafood and meat dishes in a stylish and understated setting. Brilliant desserts and attentive service. Very popular so booking essential.

RR Camel Rock, Scarborough, **T** 021-7801122. *1200-1700, 1900-2300. Map 1, I2, p247* A Mediterranean-style seafood restaurant. Sit out on the balcony and enjoy the oysters or excellent calamari, bring your own wines, good stop for lunches. Recommended.

RR Chapman's Peak Hotel, Hout Bay, **T** 021-7901036, opposite end of town to harbour. *0800-late. Map 1, E1, p246* Book in the evenings, a lively restaurant and bar.

RR Clifton Beach House, 4th Beach, Clifton, **T** 021-4381955. *0800-2300. Map 5, A1, p253* Breakfast, lunch and dinner overlooking Clifton's beautiful beach, good seafood plus some Thai dishes, relaxed during the day but more elegant at night.

RR Dunes, Hout Bay Beach, **T** 021-7901876. *1200-2200. Map 1, E1/2, p246* Sprawling restaurant overlooking the dunes behind the beach, very popular with families, large menu, quick service but the food can disappoint – stick to the tasty fish and chips.

RR Golden Dragon, 359 Main Rd, Sea Point, **T** 021-4345391. *1700-2300. Map 4, C6, p252* Full range of Chinese dishes, 'Early Bird' specials.

RR L'Orient, 50 Main Rd, Sea Point, **T** 021 4396572. *1900-2300, evenings only. Map 3, D2, p250* Indonesian and Malaysian, a popular and authentic restaurant serving a wide range of exotic dishes. The Rijsttafel has 17 individual dishes. Recommended.

RR Ocean Blue, Victoria Rd, Camps Bay, **T** 021-4389838. *1200-2200. Map 5, E3, p253* Friendly seafood restaurant on road overlooking the beach. Excellent fresh seafood, especially daily specials, superb grilled prawns and butterfish kebabs. Less pretentious than many of the restaurants in the area.

RR Red Herring, Chapman's Bay Trading Centre, Beach Rd, **T** 021-7891783. *Tue-Sun, 1200-late. Map 1, C1, p247* Excellent country cuisine, attached *Sunset* pub, but distracting sunlight from the stained glass windows.

RR San Marco, 92 Main Rd, Sea Point, **T** 021-4392758. *Wed-Mon 1900-2300. Map 3, D1, p250* A long-term favourite. Extensive Italian menu specializing in seafood. Excellent antipasto, plenty of vegetarian options, wonderful desserts. Upmarket and expensive, but worth it.

RR Wangthai, 105 Paramount Pl, **T** 021-4396164. *1130-1500, 1800-2300. Map 3, C6, p250* Great Thai restaurant serving mouth-watering stir-fries, curries with coconut milk and plenty of lemon grass. Reservations advised.

R Avanti, 341 Main Rd, Sea Point, **T** 021-4391857. *1200-2200. Map 4, C6, p252* Full range of Italian meals, good value.

R Chariots, 107 Main Rd, Green Point, **T** 021-4345427. *1000-2200. Map 3, D8, p251* Excellent local Italian restaurant serving tradi-tional and innovative pasta dishes (try the curried butternut ravi-oli), superb risotto, salads and meat dishes. Low-key and relaxed, good service, tables overlooking Main Rd, popular with young pro-fessionals. Excellent value for money. Recommended.

Cafés

R Café Erté, 265 Main Rd, Sea Point, **T** 021-4346624. *0800-late. Map 3, D2, p250* Trendy café playing loud trance and techno, good breakfasts and snacks, internet access.

R Dirty Dick's Tavern, Harbour Rd, Hout Bay, **T** 021-7905609. *1100-late. Map 1, E1, p246* Beer garden and restaurant with open-air terrace overlooking the marina. Steaks, fish and salads.

R Fish on the Rocks, Harbour Rd (beyond Snoekies Market), Hout Bay, **T** 021-7901153. *1000-2100. Map 1, E1, p246* Simple and delicious fresh fish and chips, no frills. Recommended.

A room with a view

Dining out, enjoying great views, is par for the course in Cape Town.

R **Oven Door**, Main Rd, Hout Bay. *0800-1800. Map 1, E1/2, p246* Breakfast and lunch. A very popular street café next to some curio shops and the information centre, unfortunately location on the main road suffers from fumes especially during holiday months.

R **News Café**, corner Main Dr and Ashstead Rd, Green Point, T 021-9197490. *1000-late. Map 3, D7, p251* Popular café and bar serving sandwiches, salads, pub meals, stylish decor, gets busy in the evenings.

R **New York Bagels**, 51 Regent Rd, Sea Point, T 021-4397523. *0700-2100. Map 4, F3, p252* Cafeteria-style deli serving a good range of food, from hearty American breakfasts and smoked salmon bagels through to salads, hotdogs and fish and chips. Attached deli shop next door sells bagels to take away.

R **Rumblin' Tum**, Shoreline Centre, Hout Bay, T 021-7902047. *0900-1700. Map 1, E1/2, p246* Family coffee shop and restaurant serving good breakfasts (delicious muesli and yoghurt), but small portions. Mix of light lunches, outside terrace, sluggish service.

R **Marc's Deli Bar**, Shop 16, The Promenade, Camps Bay, T 021-4382322. *0700-1900. Map 5, E3, p253* Smart first-floor deli and café overlooking beach, serving wonderful pastries, muffins and cakes as well as selling a fine selection of breads and cheeses.

Southern suburbs

Restaurants

RRR **Au Jardin**, Vineyard Hotel, Colinton Rd, Newlands, T 021-6831520. *1200-1400, 1900-2200, closed Sun, Mon and Jul. Map 1, C4, p246* A very smart hotel restaurant with one of the best

French menus in Cape Town. Six-course meals or a quick plat du jour served in a stylish setting with views of the mountain. Polite service, excellent presentation. The best local ingredients turned into the best European recipes. Recommended. Booking advised.

RRR Buitenverwachting, Klein Constantia Rd, Constantia, **T** 021-7943522. *Tue-Sat 1200-1400, 1900-2200. Map 1, D3, p246* One of the best restaurants in Cape Town, flawless Italian and French cuisine, good service, upmarket, prices reflect the quality of the food.

RRR The Cellars, The Cellars-Hohenort Hotel, 93 Brommersvlei Rd, Constantia, **T** 021-7942137. *1200-1400, 1800-2300. Map 1, D3, p246* A highly praised menu which might be too trendy for some palates. The restaurant is in an exclusive five-star hotel. A little too formal for a fun night out, but still one of the best hotel-based restaurants in the area.

RRR La Colombe, Constantia Uitsig, Constantia, **T** 021-7942390. *Closed Tue and Sun evening, Jul and Aug. Map 1, D3, p246* Excellent French menu with strong Provençal flavours. Delicious fresh fish and a range of meat and duck dishes, with an emphasis on rich sauces. During fine weather you can sit outside and look over the gardens and a pool.

RRR Fiamma's, 23-25 Wolf St, Wynberg, **T** 021-7616175. *Lunch 1200-1400 Tue-Fri. Dinner Mon-Sat. 1900-2300. Map 1, D4, p246* Smart new Italian restaurant serving fine traditional dishes with a South African twist. Friendly service, attractive surrounds.

RRR Parks, 114 Constantia Rd, Constantia, **T** 021-7978202. *Closed Mon. Map 1, D3, p246* Enjoy a drink in the lounge before moving into one of the two dining areas overlooking a colourful garden. Broad range of well-presented dishes, making good use of fresh local produce. Mostly traditional dishes, plenty for vegetarians, excellent service. Recommended.

RRR Steenberg, Steenberg Country Hotel, Spaanschemat River Rd, Constantia, **T** 021-7132222. *1200-1500, 1900 late. Map 1, D3, p246* The principal restaurant in a five-star hotel. Tables are set in cosy alcoves created from old wine vats. An expensive and smart place to dine out, but like many hotel restaurants lacks a spontaneous character. International menu designed to satisfy the tastes of hotel guests from all over the world.

RR Barrister's Grill, corner of Kildare and Main St, Newlands, **T** 021-6741792. *0800-late. Map 1, C4, p246* A popular steakhouse that has expanded into a trendy bistro/café during the day with plenty of alfresco tables. Still retains the Mock-Tudor timber decor of the steakhouse. Plenty for vegetarians.

RR Kirstenbosch Restaurant, Kirstenbosch Botanical Gardens, **T** 021-7998783. *1200-2200. Map 1, D3, p246* Stunning setting at the bottom of the gardens, with views up towards Table Mountain. Fairly pricey but good meals, including Cape specialities such as bobotie, plus salads, steaks and pasta. Friendly service.

RR Rory's, Lower Main Rd, Observatory, **T** 021-4488301. *1900-late. Map 7, C4, p255* Stylish and homely restaurant run by chef Rory, menu changes daily, excellent fresh ingredients with a fusion twist, relaxed setting and trendy crowd.

R Don Pedro's, 113 Roodebloem Rd, Woodstock, **T** 021-4474493, info@donpedro.co.za *1100-late. Map 6, B7, p254* Informal, bustling restaurant serving huge portions of South African food, pasta and pizza at cheap prices. Very popular, focal point of the community, great mixed crowd, book ahead. Recommended.

R **Fratelli**, Cavendish Sq, Claremont, **T** 021-6836018. *1000-2200. Map 1, C4, p246* Set in popular food court, cheerful good-value pasta and steaks.

R **Mango**, Cavendish Sq, Claremont, **T** 021-6741350. *1200-2200. Map 1, C4, p246* Friendly place serving a mix of South African and US-style food, ribs, stews, seafood, burgers. Good spot to fill up before seeing a film upstairs.

R **Pancho's**, Lower Main Rd, Observatory, **T** 021-4474854. *1200-2100. Map 7, A3, p255* Mexican dishes in a lively atmosphere, all the usual tacos and fajitas, good home made nachos, nothing fancy but a fun place. Tasty cocktails.

Cafés

R **Juicy Lucy**, Link Centre, Claremont, **T** 021-6717407. *0800-late. Map 1, C4, p246* Coffee shop and juice bar, good toasted sandwiches, fresh juices and milkshakes.

R **Marigolds**, 5 Grove Av, Claremont, **T** 021 6744670. *1100-1600. Map 1, C4, p246* One of the few vegetarian restaurants in town, usual selection of quiche, soups and salads, closed evenings, no smoking.

R **Nino's**, Cavendish Sq, Claremont, **T** 021-6837288. *1200-2100. Map 1, C4, p246* Popular haunt for shoppers to rest up and try one of Nino's delicious toasted paninis, salads or pasta dishes.

R **Obz Café**, 115 Lower Main Rd, Observatory, **T** 021-4485555. *0800-late. Map 7, B3, p255* Popular place open all day for light meals, coffee or cocktails, great salads and sandwiches, some tables on pavement outside.

False Bay

Restaurants

RRR Black Marlin, Miller's Point, 2 km from Simon's Town,
T 021-7861621. *1100-1500. Map 1, I3, p247* Sea views and a wide range of fresh seafood, excellent crayfish, comprehensive wine list. Recommended, although it can get very busy with tour buses in summer.

RRR Bon Appetit, 90 St George's St, Simon's Town,
T 021-7862412. *1200-1500, 1900-2300, closed Mon. Map 1, I3, p247* One of the best restaurants in the area. Excellent French menu, very fresh ingredients, simple seafood and meat dishes, popular, book ahead.

RRR Horatio's, Lord Nelson Inn, Simon's Town, **T** 021-7861386.
1900-2200. Map 1, I3, p247 This is the hotel's smarter restaurant, serving good but pricey seafood and roasts.

RR Bay View Galley, on the beach at Fish Hoek,
T 021-7823354. *1200-late. Map 1, G3, p247* Serves continental dishes and a good choice of fresh seafood. Recommended.

RR Bertha's, Quayside Centre, Wharf Rd, Simon's Town,
T 021-7862138. *1100-2300. Map 1, I3, p247* A seafood grill and coffee house in the centre of town in a prime location overlooking the yacht harbour. During the day the outside terrace is a good place to enjoy good fresh seafood and watch the goings on in the harbour. Inside is a dining area perfect for large family meals. Great selection of fresh seafood dishes, good value. Recommended.

★ **Child-friendly restaurants**

Best

- Dunes, Hout Bay, p145
- Bertha's, Simon's Town, p152
- Penguin Point Café, Boulders Beach, p154
- Jonkerhuis, Groot Constantia, p74
- Fish on the Rocks, Hout Bay, p146

RR Café Pescado, 118 St George's St (opposite Jubilee Square), Simon's Town, **T** 021-7862272. *1100-2200. Map 1, I3, p247*
A popular family set-up serving some of the best seafood along the coast. Try the calamari and always check what the catch of the day is. Recommended.

RR Cape to Cuba, Main Rd, Kalk Bay, **T** 021-7883695. *1200-1600, 1900-late. Map 1, G3, p247* Atmospheric Cuban restaurant and cocktail bar serving good-value seafood with a Caribbean edge. Great setting on the water's edge with tables overlooking the harbour, funky decor, enjoyable Cuban music.

RR Dixies, 143 Main Rd, Simon's Town. **T** 021-7862105. *1800-2300. Map 1, I3, p247* Indonesian and Dutch meals.

RR Gaylords, 65 Main Rd, Muizenberg, **T** 021-7885470. *Wed-Sun 1200-1500, 1800-2300. Map 1, F3, p246* Excellent Indian meals, recommended for seafood and vegetarian dishes.

RR Hardy's in the Lord Nelson Inn, Simon's Town, **T** 021-7861386. *1200-1600. Map 1, I3, p247* Excellent informal lunchtime pub meals.

RR Mykonos, Main Rd, Kalk Bay, **T** 021-4392106. *1700-late. Map 1, I3, p247* Authentic Greek food, friendly service.

RR Penguin Point Café, Boulders Beach, **T** 021-7861758.
0700-late. Map 1, I3, p247 Open for breakfasts through to dinner.
Excellent restaurant with bar and sundeck which is always busy
with day-trippers. Good English breakfasts, cocktails (including the
popular Pickled Penguins), and meals made from fresh ingredients
with a slight experimental feel to them. Try the salads during the
day and the fresh fish by night.

RR Plymouth Sound, **T** 021-7862993, Runciman's Building,
St George's St, Simon's Town. *0800-1800. Map 1, I3, p247* Good
breakfasts and snacks, check the daily specials, comfortable
old-style setting.

RR Railway House, Railway Station, Muizenberg,
T 021-7883251. *1200-1500, 1900-2200, closed Sun evening. Map 1,
F4, p246* Newly refurbished restaurant, friendly service, seafood
and steaks (including ostrich).

RR The Timeless Way, 106 Main Rd, Kalk Bay, **T/F** 021-7885619.
1100-1400, 1900-late. Map 1, G3, p246 An excellent restaurant
serving Cape cuisine, steaks and seafood. Ronny and Kelly ensure a
high standard of service. Recommended.

R The Brass Bell, **T** 021-7885455, by the railway station in Kalk
Bay. *1200-late. Map 1, G3, p246* A well-known and very popular
restaurant, young clientele, gets very busy around sunset. Great
location right by the waves, simple set-up serving pub meals and
good fresh fish and chips, great for a cool beer outside close to
the waves.

R Salty Sea Dog, next to Quayside Centre, Simon's Town.
1200-1700. Map 1, I3, p247 Cheap and cheerful place serving fresh
fish and chips with seats overlooking the harbour.

Cafés

R Caribbean Coffee Company, Quayside, Simon's Town, **T** 021-4480316. *1000-1800. Map 1, I3, p247* Sandwiches, salads and filled pancakes, tables overlooking the harbour, good coffee, nice place for lunch.

R Mediterraneo, Quayside Centre, Simon's Town. *0800-1800. Map 1, I3, p247* Homemade soups, cakes and deli. Breezy setting, great for afternoon snacks.

R Olympia Café, 138 Main Rd, Kalk Bay, **T** 021-7886396. *0700-1700. Map 1, G3, p247* Hugely popular café and deli serving up breakfast, soups, sandwiches and more substantial meals at lunchtime.

R We Live Like This, Main Rd, Kalk Bay. *0800-2000. Map 1, G3, p247* Stylish deli and kitchen shop that sells sandwiches and healthy snacks.

R Whalers Tavern, York Rd, Muizenberg. *1100 late. Map 1, F4, p246* A lively pub serving snack meals, all the usual trappings for a rowdy drinking night, views across False Bay.

The Winelands

Stellenbosch

RRR Vinkel en Koljander, Lanzerac Manor, **T** 021-8871132. *1130-1600. Map 8, E2/3, p256* Light lunches and country dishes, with a terrace.

RRR De Volkskombuis, Old Strand Rd, **T** 021-8872121.
1200-1500, 1900-2100, closed Sun evening. Map 8, E2/3, p256 A
high standard of food and service, specialities are Cape dishes with
strong European influences. Try the home-made oxtail or
springbok pies. The atmosphere is enhanced by the character of
the building, a restored Herbert Baker Cape Dutch homestead,
with views across the Eerste River. A sensibly priced treat.

RR The Coachman, Ryneveld St, next to Village Museum.
1100-1430, 1700-2200. Map 8, E2/3, p256 Beer garden serving
light meals and snacks, nice setting, popular with tour groups.

RR Decameron, 50 Plein St, **T** 021-8833331. *1200-late. Map 8,
E2/3, p256* Italian cuisine, decent pasta, beer garden under vines.

RR Doornbosch, Old Strand Rd, **T** 021-8875079. *1200-1500,
1800-late, closed Sun evening. Map 8, E2/3, p256* Italian and French
dishes, served in a long thatched cottage set in beautiful gardens,
the perfect spot during the summer, popular, booking advisable.
Recommended.

RR Fishmonger, Sanlam Bldg, c/o Plein and Ryneveld sts,
T 021-8877835. *1200-1400, 1800-late. Map 8, E2/3, p256* A very
popular seafood restaurant, sensibly priced, good service, booking
essential. Recommended.

RR Mamma Roma, Vredenheim Estate, R310, **T** 021-8813001.
1100-2200. Map 8, E2, p256 Essentially Italian plus seafood from
the Cape, recently relocated to this winery.

RR Mexican Kitchen, 25 Bird St, **T** 021-8829997. *1200-2300.
Map 8, E2/3, p256* Great new cantina-style restaurant serving huge
portions of nachos, bean soup, fajitas, tacos and steaks. Relaxed
setting with inventive decor – some of the seats are swings.

RR Midnite Grill, 59 Plein St. *Map 8, E2/3, p256* Late night venue.

RR Spice Café, 34 Kerkstraat. *0900-1800. Map 8, E2/3, p256* Cosy eccentric place with a garden, serving simple tasty meals.

R Blue Orange, Dorp St, **T** 021-8864014. *0800-1800. Map 8, E2/3, p256* Excellent breakfasts, good value snacks and sandwiches, popular with students.

R Café Nouveau, Plein St. *0800-2000. Map 8, E2/3, p256* Lovely old-fashioned café serving sandwiches, coffee and cakes.

R Dros, corner of Bird and Alexander sts, **T** 021-8864856. *1100-late. Map 8, E2/3, p256* A large bar-cum-restaurant with plenty of outdoor seating in a lively square. Popular chain serving standard pub fare such as burgers, steaks and pizza. Good value, but portions are on the small side.

R Evergreen, 5 Plein St. *0800-1730, closed Sun. Map 8, E2/3, p256* Breakfasts and light vegetarian meals.

R Panarottis, Bird St. *1200-late. Map 8, E2/3, p256* Pizza, pasta and juice bar, take-aways, good value and popular high street chain.

R Ha!Ha!, Ryneveld St, opposite Village Museum. *0930-1900. Map 8, E2/3, p256* Good place to stop for a cool drink or coffee and cake after visiting the museum.

Franschhoek

RRR La Couronne, Robertsvlei Rd, **T** 021-8762770. *1200-1430, 1830-2200. Map 8, E6, p256* Small, formal restaurant in a smart hotel, perfect setting among vines. Light lunches, five-course dinners, excellent local and international dishes.

RRR La Maison de Chamonix, 1 Uitkyk St, **T** 021-8762393. *1100-1500, 1800-late, closed Mon.* *Map 8, E6, p256* Upmarket country-style on the wine estate, good vegetarian menu.

RRR Monneaux, Main Rd, **T** 021-8763386. *1230-1430, 1830-late.* *Map 8, E6, p256* Contemporary fusion cuisine, more up-to-date than many restaurants in Franschhoek, attractive outdoor terrace and cosy dining room.

RRR Le Quartier Français, 16 Huguenot Rd, **T** 021-8762151. *1200-1400, 1900-2300.* *Map 8, E6, p256* Rated as one of the best restaurants in the Western Cape. Expensive French and South African dishes, rather fussy and over-rated, but nevertheless a nice place for a treat.

RR Le Ballon Rouge, 12 Reservoir St, **T** 021-8762651. *1200-late.* *Map 8, E6, p256* Next to the guesthouse, sensibly priced meals made from fresh local produce, not your typical South African fare. Its deserved success has made this a popular restaurant, but when full it lacks the intimate and peaceful ambience of elsewhere in the village.

RR Bijoux, 58 Huguenot Rd, **T** 021-8763474. *1230-1500, 1800-late.* *Map 8, E6, p256* Relaxed bistro serving grills, seafood, good oysters, outdoor terrace, very popular.

RR Chez Michel, Huguenot Rd, **T** 021-8762671. *1730-2200.* *Map 8, E6, p256* A small easy-paced restaurant, good selection of imaginative dishes, rather over-the-top decor.

RR Dominic's, 66 Huguenot Rd, **T** 021-8762255. *1100-2200.* *Map 8, E6, p256* Easy-going country pub serving hearty meals, enjoy the shady gardens in the summer and the log fire in the winter, next to the information office.

RR The Grapevine, Huguenot Rd, **T** 021-8762520. *1200 1500, 1800-2200. Map 8, E6, p256* Recommended for fish and game braais.

RR Mountain View, Excelsior Rd, **T** 021-8762071. *1130-1500, 1730-late. Map 8, E6, p256* Large restaurant in Franschhoek Mountain Manor, plenty of tables in the garden, vegetarian menu, popular for Sunday lunch, booking advised during holiday season.

RR La Petite Fêrme, Pass Rd, 2 km out of town, **T** 021-8763016. *1200-1400, 1800-2130. Map 8, E6, p256* Local trout and lamb, vegetarian menu, good views of the valley, especially in the autumn. Recommended.

R Le Rendezvous, Huguenot Rd. *0900-1700. Map 8, E6, p256* Restaurant and coffee shop located in the Oude Stallen Centre, peaceful outdoor terrace, light meals and traditional dishes.

Paarl

RRR Bosman's, Grande Roche Hotel, Plantasie St, **T** 021-8632727. *1200-1400, 1830-2100. Map 8, B4, p256* International cuisine of the highest standard, imaginative vegetarian menu, huge selection of wines, all the trappings of a luxury hotel.

RRR Laborie, Taillefert St, **T** 021-8073095. *1200-1500, 1800-2200. Map 8, C4, p256* Restaurant on the wine estate, Cape and Mediterranean dishes, quite smart but relaxed atmosphere, good service.

RR Boschendal, Pniel Rd, **T** 021-8704211. *Lunch 1230-1500, café 1000-1700. Map 8, B4, p256* Picnic hampers in a lovely rural setting from November to April. Also a café and restaurant serving a cellar buffet. The vegetarian menu is exceptionally good for the country. The manor house was once the home of Cecil Rhodes.

RR Kontreihuis, 193 Main St (in *Zomerlust* guesthouse), T 021-8722808. *1200-1500, 1830-2200. Map 8, B4, p256* Traditional Cape meals served in an attractive dining room, the sort of place where you are liable to linger after enjoying your meal.

RR Pontac, 16 Zion St (in *Pontac* guesthouse), T 021-8720445. *1200-1400, 1900-late. Map 8, B4, p256* Informal and stylish restaurant serving traditional dishes, with a 'New World' flair.

RR Rhebokskloof, Rhebokskloof Estate, T 021-8638606, restaurant@rhebokskloof *Mon-Sat, 1200-1600, Thu-Mon 1830-2200. Map 8, B4, p256* Excellent restaurant serving simple traditional fare as well as fancier international dishes, excellent wine list, attractive surroundings.

RR Spring Fontein, Dal Kosafat, T 021-8682808. *1200-1400, 1800-late. Map 8, B4, p256* Traditional South African dishes served on a veranda with pretty views.

RR Wagon Wheels, 57 Lady Grey St, T 021-8725265. *1130-1500, 1800-2200. Map 8, B4, p256* Popular upmarket steakhouse serving excellent steaks and a small selection of fish dishes and salads.

R Dros, Main Rd, T 021-8864856. *1100-late. Map 8, B4, p256* Outlet of successful chain serving steaks, ribs and pasta dishes in a cellar atmosphere. Also has a good choice of beers at the bar.

R Kostenrighting, 19 Pastorie Av. *0900-1700. Map 8, B4, p256* Coffee shop serving light meals, sandwiches and coffee and cakes, tables in the dappled shade of oak trees.

R Pasadena Spur, Main St, T 021-8729553. *1100-2300. Map 8, B4, p256* Good value steakhouse, salad bars, lively, part of a very popular chain.

The Whale Coast

Hermanus

RRR The Burgundy, 16 Harbour Rd, **T** 028-3122800. *1200-1530, 1700-2200, closed Mon*. Restored rural cottage by the sea. One of the top restaurants in town but very relaxed and good value, with tables spilling onto a shady terrace outside. Excellent seafood including superb grilled crayfish.

RR Bientang's Cave, access via steps from the car park on Marine Drive between the village square and Marine Hotel, **T** 028-3123454. *1230 1430, 1800-late, closed Wed out of season*. The name doesn't lie – the venue is an actual cave. Excellent seafood buffets, simple wood benches and long tables, very popular, book ahead.

RR Fisherman's Cottage, Old Harbour, **T** 028-3123642. *1200-late, closed Sun*. Tiny place serving excellent seafood, simple dishes such as seafood potjie, charming setting. Choose a veranda table in good weather. Known as the smallest pub in town.

RR Mogg's Country Cookhouse, **T** 028-3124321. *By appointment only. Lunches Wed-Sun, evening meals Fri and Sat only. Situated in the Hemel-en-Aarde Valley, 12 km from Hermanus centre. Take the R43 out of town for Cape Town, after 2 km turn onto the R320 for Caledon*. The restaurant is run by Jenny and her daughter, Julia, who prepare a seasonal menu. Every dish is freshly prepared and served in a lovely rustic setting. Recommended.

RR Ocean Basket, Fashion Sq, Main Rd, **T** 028-3121529.
1100-2300. The usual good, fresh seafood you can expect from this chain. Good value, quick meals.

RR Ouzeri, 60 St Peter's Lane, **T** 028-3130532. *1200-2300, closed Sun afternoon and Mon*. Greek taverna, lively atmosphere, tasty vegetarian dishes plus the usual Greek fare, fully licensed.

R Charlie's Tapas, Market Sq, **T** 028-3130110. *1130-late*.
Light meals, and tapas-type snacks in a lively pub atmosphere.

R Flavour of Italy, Main Rd, opposite Marine Hotel,
T 028-3122137. *0800-1830*. Coffee shop and deli, also serves light pasta lunches.

R Prince of Whales, Astoria Village, **T** 028-3130725. *0730-1600*.
Excellent breakfasts, pancakes and fresh croissants.

R The Fish Shoppe, Market Sq, **T** 028-3121819. *0900-1730*.
Simple seafood restaurant and tackle shoo, good value fish and chips and calamari.

R Rossi's, 10 High St, **T** 028-3122848. *Open daily*.
Evening takeaway service, Italian dishes, good value steaks.

R San Remo Spur, 38 Main Rd, **T** 028-3121915. *1130-2300*.
Good value steak meals, popular as all outlets are in this chain.

Cape Town's nightlife scene is huge and you'll find a thumping bar on just about any night of the week. Saturday nights are the biggest, followed closely by Wednesdays, when Capetonians hit the bars and let their hair down after work. While bars are always free to get in, clubs usually charge an entry fee – generally from about R10, up to R40. In typical Cape Town style, opening hours are far from strict and you'll be hard pressed to find a place which closes before you're ready to call it a night. Bars tend to fill up from around 1800, while clubs are virtually deserted before midnight, and techno clubs stay open until well into the next morning. Some bars, as the night progresses, end up becoming 'clubs' so check out both sets of listings.

Long Street is one of the main areas and is lined with bars, cafés and small clubs, and is popular with backpackers and fashionable, young locals. The main gay scene is at Green Point where there are excellent bars and clubs along the main road (see also p169). Observatory is the city's alternative hub, with laidback bars and cutting-edge clubs.

Music is central to a night out and people get quite passionate about their tunes. You'll mostly hear mainstream house, but techno is popular, drum 'n' bass, hip-hop and Latin sounds. You should also hear Kwaito, a relaxed form of house with booming bass – the dance music from young, black Jo'burg. Kwaito is the biggest movement in music at the moment, but young white and coloured people are only just getting into it. There are a number of large-scale events held in and around Cape Town – popular nights include Vortex and Alien Safari – pure techno. Look out for flyers in bars and cafés. *The Cape Times* and *Argus* have good listings sections, as does *Cape Review* magazine. Otherwise, check out www.clubbersguide.co.za

The city centre

Bars

Cool Runnings, 108 Kloof St, Gardens, **T** 021-4248388. *Daily 1100-late. Map 2, F3, p248* One of Kloof Street's most popular drinking holes. With a beach-bar themed deck and pub meals, it always gets packed at weekends with a lively throng.

Dros, Kloof St, Gardens, **T** 021-4236800. *Daily 1200-late. Map 2, C5, p248* Busy pub and bar serving standard pub fare, wine cellar decor, nice tables overlooking the street. Popular bar serving light meals and featuring communal drumming sessions. Grab a drum and join in, or watch the professionals on Friday and Saturday nights.

The Lounge, 194 Long St. *Mon-Sat 2000-0200. R20. Map 2, B6, p248* Fashionable bar and club with several small rooms, big sofas, house music most nights, drum 'n' bass on Wed, great balcony overlooking Long Street.

Jo'burg, 218 Long St, **T** 021-4220241. *Daily 1500-0300. Map 2, B6, p248* Trendy bar serving pints and cocktails to a mixed crowd, gay-friendly, relaxed during the week but gets very busy at weekends when DJs spin funky house and drum 'n' bass. One of the best in the area.

Kennedy's Cigar Bar, 251 Long St, **T** 021-4241212. *Daily 1700-late. Map 2, B6, p248* Upmarket cigar and cocktail lounge, old-fashioned brass-and-wood decor, daily live jazz, mature well-heeled crowd.

Mama Africa, 178 Long St, **T** 021-4248634. *Mon-Sat 1900-late. R10, free if you're eating. Map 2, B6, p248* Great live music every night, usually Marimba. Part of the popular restaurant, the bar is smallish with a long, wood-carved green mamba making up the bar. Limited seating, great atmosphere, quite touristy.

Perseverance Tavern, 83 Buitenkant St, **T** 021-4612440. *Daily from lunch-late. Map 2, D8, p249* Cape Town's oldest pub, pub food available in two dining rooms, beer garden, plenty of drinking corners, full on at the weekend, good Sunday roast lunch, live music.

Poo Na Na Souk Bar, Heritage Sq, 100 Shortmarket St, **T** 021-4234889. *1700-late. Map 3, H10, p251* Ultra-trendy bar decked out in Moroccan lanterns and expensive fabrics, lovely balconies overlooking the even trendier *Strega* restaurant, usually relaxed atmosphere but sometimes host big-name international DJs.

Purple Turtle Pub, Long St, **T** 021-4236194. *Daily 1100-late. Map 2, A7, p249* Grotty pub which remains very popular, with a large, dark interior dotted with TV screens. Pub lunches, pool tables, live bands on Sat. Virtual Turtle is their internet café spin-off, found upstairs and around the city.

★ **Most up for-it venues**

Be st
- Vacca Matta, Foreshore, p168
- The Green Man, Claremont, p172
- Angels, Green Point, p209.
- 169, Long Street, p167
- The Bronx, Green Point, p169

Clubs

169, 169 Long St, **T** 021-4261107. *Thu, Fri and Sat 1900-late. R20. Map 2, B7, p249* R&B club with a lively, mixed crowd, some Kwaito. Fairly small venue, with a great balcony overlooking busy Long Street. Gets packed on Fridays.

Club More, 74 Loop St, **T** 021-4220544. *Wed-Sat 2200-late. R20. Map 3, H10, p251* Popular large-scale dance venue playing garage, house and techno.

Dharma Club, 68 Kloof St, Gardens, **T** 021-4220909, www.the dharmaclub.com *Daily 1700-late. Map 2, D4, p248* Small, trendy bar with vaguely Asian decor. Intimate setting and excellent music mixed by a live DJ, good fusion meals, but an over-dressed, pretentious crowd.

D-lite, Loop St, **T** 021-2216038. *Late starter. Map 2, A7, p249* House sounds with a factory interior.

The Fez, 38 Hout St, **T** 021-4231456, www.fez.co.za *1800-late. R40. Map 2, A8, p249* Moroccan-themed interior, young and well-heeled crowd, funky house and themed parties.

Bars and clubs

Vacca Matta, Seeff House, Foreshore, **T** 021-4195550. *Wed-Sat, 1900-late. R20.* Full on drinking haunt and cramped club with waitresses dancing on the bar, 'ladies' get in for cheap and often get free cocktails, seriously tacky but resolutely popular.

Victoria and Alfred Waterfront

Bars

Den Anker, Victoria & Alfred Pierhead, **T** 021-4190249. *Daily 1100-0100. Map 3, C11, p251* Belgian restaurant and bar specializing in a range of Belgian draught and bottled beers.

Quay Four, **T** 021-4192008. *Daily 1100-late. Map 3, B11, p251* Large shady deck overlooking the water, popular with well-heeled locals and tourists, good meals and great draught beer, one of the more pleasant pubs on the Waterfront.

Ferryman's Tavern, next to the amphitheatre, Waterfront, **T** 021-4197748. *Daily 1100-0100. Map 3, C10, p251* A popular haunt with restaurant upstairs, outside seating, TV continually showing sports action, the olives and feta go well with the Mitchell's Beer brewed on site, a low-key crowd.

Sports Café, Victoria Wharf, **T** 021-4195558. *Daily 1100-late. Map 3, B11, p251* Sports bar showing matches on big screens, rowdy atmosphere and a mostly white, rugby-playing clientele.

Clubs

Cantina Tequila, Quay 5, Victoria Wharf, **T** 021-4190207. *Daily, 1100-late, R20 after 2300. Map 3, B11, p251* This Mexican restaurant transforms into a packed nightclub after about 2300, mostly chart music, popular with tourists.

Atlantic Seaboard

Bars

Bosa Nova, Somerset Rd, Green Point. *1700-late. Map 3, F10, p251* Large bar with seats overlooking the street, vague tropical theme, small dance floor at the back, pop and house music.

The Bronx, 35 Somerset Rd, corner Napier St, Green Point, **T** 021-4212779, www.bronx.co.za *Daily 1900-late. Map 3, F10, p251* Very popular gay bar and club with tiny main bar, plus two others, gets packed out at weekends, mostly men but women welcome, live DJs spin out thumping techno.

Buena Vista Social Café, Main Rd, Green Point, **T** 021-4330611. *1200-late, R30 after 2200. Map 3, D7, p251* Cuban-themed bar and restaurant catering to a well-heeled crowd. Latin music, live bands at weekend, tasteful decor and a relaxed atmosphere, nice balcony, great spot for sophisticated cocktails on a hot evening.

Café Caprice, Victoria Rd, Camps Bay, **T** 021-4388315. *Daily 1200-2300. Map 5, E4, p253* Popular café and bar with outdoor seats overlooking the beach, great fresh-fruit cocktails, beautiful, well-heeled crowd, gets packed at sunset.

Chilli 'n' Lime, 23 Somerset Rd, Green Point, **T** 082-2582382. *2100-late. R40. Map 3, F10, p251* Trendy bar and club spread over two floors, with mirrored walls, stylish lighting and a tiny dance floor. Pretentious, over-priced and very young, but playing good hip-hop on Saturday nights.

Dizzy Jazz Café, 41 The Drive, Camps Bay, **T** 021-4382686. *Daily, 1200-0100. Map 5, E4, p253* Busy bar and live music venue, popular jazz nights at the weekend, wide terrace with sea views.

La Med, Glen Country Club, Victoria Rd, Clifton, **T** 021-4385600, www.lamed.co.za *Tue-Sun, 1100-late. Map 5, D4, p253* Popular meeting place for Cape Town's young, white and well-off, busy bar next to the rocks and overlooking the sea, plenty of seats spilling out of the interior, good pub food, great for a sundowner, turns into a raucous club later on.

Sandbar, Victoria Rd, Camps Bay, no telephone. *Tue-Sun, 1100-2300. Map 5, D4, p253* Popular for sundowners, café serving light meals during the day, shady tables on the pavement opposite the beach.

Skebanga's, Red Herring, Noordhoek, **T** 021-7891783. *Tue-Sun, 1100-0100. Map 1, F2, p246* Outdoor deck with great views, upmarket pub atmosphere with an older, well-dressed crowd. Sports events screened.

Tuscany Beach Café, Victoria Rd, Camps Bay, **T** 021-4381213. *Daily 1100-2300. Map 5, E3, p253* Minimalist interior, good bar snacks, laid-back and trendy crowd.

Clubs

Angels, 27 Somerset Rd, Green Point, **T** 021-4198547. *Wed, Fri, Sat, 2200-late. R20. Map 3, F10, p251* One of the most popular gay clubs in town, with a pleasant outdoor courtyard and bar leading onto a huge dance floor. Friendly, unpretentious crowd, mostly house and techno plus some cheesy tunes.

Club 55, Somerset Rd, Green Point, **T** 021-4251849, www.55.co.za *Daily 1100-late (opens 2100 on cabaret nights). R20. Map 3, F10, p251* Popular gay club, seats on pavement lead to busy dance floor inside, well-known DJs spin trance and progressive house on Friday and Saturday, cabaret on Tuesday, Thursday and Sunday.

S.K.Y, Napier St, Green Point, **T** 021-4198547. *Fri and Sat, 2100-late. Map 3, F10, p251* Fashionable dance complex, industrial interior, two dance floors, four bars, courtyard with outside bar, mixed crowd, mostly techno and progressive house.

Southern Suburbs

Bars

Bijou, Lower Main Rd, Observatory, **T** 021-4480183. *Tue-Sun, 2000-late. R15-30 after 2200. Map 7, A3, p255* New ultra-trendy bar/club/theatre very popular with an arty pack, weekly fashion shows, plays, gigs and parties held in a huge open-air concrete theatre on the roof, dancing area on second floor, groovy bar on ground floor, great cocktails. Expect to pay an entry fee after 2200 or have a personal invite.

Café Ganesh, Trill Rd, Observatory, **T** 021-4483435. *1200-0100. Map 7, A4, p255* Lively little café and bar serving hearty Cape dishes and ice-cold beers in a leafy courtyard leading to a characterful interior. Very friendly, great place to meet local Obs characters.

Forrester's Arms, Newlands Av, **T** 021-6895949. *Daily 1100-late. Map 7, F4, p255* A favourite with students, especially sports jocks. Standard pub with a fun-loving, boozy scene.

The Green Man, Main Rd, Claremont. *Daily 1100-late. Map 1, C4, p246* Most popular bar in Claremont despite its grim, modern interior. Very young, pint-quaffing crowd, small dancing area, mostly rock music, often frequented by Springbok players.

Keg & Grouse, Riverside Centre, Rondebosch, **T** 021-6893000. *Daily 1100-late. Map 1, C4, p246* English-style pub serving bar meals, popular with local students and older sporty types.

Sports Café, Atrium Centre, Claremont, **T** 021-6741152. *1100-late. Map 1, C4, p246* Popular second floor bar showing all the important games on big screen TVs, tacky, busy balcony.

A Touch of Madness, Pepper Tree Sq, Nuttal Rd, Observatory, **T** 021-4482266. *Daily 1500-late. Map 7, B4, p255* Flamboyant bar with series of rooms decked out with tongue-in-cheek opulence, eccentric regulars, great atmosphere, good light meals.

Clubs

Independent Armchair Theatre, 135 Lower Main Rd, Observatory, **T** 021-4471514. *Daily 2000-0100. From R12 depending on what's on. Map 7, A3, p255* Popular small-scale venue with huge sofas to lounge in, featuring films on Monday, jazz on Thursday, live bands most nights, excellent stand-up comedy from the Cape Comedy Collective on Sunday. Recommended.

False Bay

Bars

The Brass Bell, by the train station in Kalk Bay, **T** 021-7882943. *Daily 1100-late. Map 1, G3, p247* Popular pub set right on the waves, great spot for a cold beer watching the sunset. Young, noisy crowd. Live music at weekends.

Cape to Cuba, Main Rd, Kalk Bay, **T** 021-7883695. *Tue-Sat, 1200-2300. Map 1, G3, p247* Atmospheric Cuban restaurant which turns into a cocktail bar later on, great drinks, lovely tables looking across the harbour, the Cuban music makes a nice change from the usual rock or house.

Harbourside Pub, 136 Main Rd, Kalk Bay. *Daily 1100-2400. Map 1, G3, p247* Old-fashioned and pleasant pub on the first floor with a great balcony overlooking Main Rd and the harbour. Good meals, live music – usually jazz – at weekends.

The Two and Sixpence, Main Rd, Simon's Town, *next to British Hotel*, **T** 021-7861371. *Daily 1100-2300. Map 1, I3, p247* Friendly, old-style bar with pool tables, pub food, range of beers.

Wipeout Bar, corner Camp and Main rds, Muizenberg, **T** 021-7884803. *Daily 1700-late. Map 1 F4, p246* Large tropical-themed bar, popular with backpackers and surfers, pub food, cocktails, live music at weekends.

Stellenbosch

Bars

Bohemia Pub, Ryneveld St, **T** 021-8828375. *1200-late. Map 8, F2/3, p256* One of the relaxed student haunts, serving snacks.

Dros, corner of Bird and Alexander sts, **T** 021-8864856. *1000-late. Map 8, E2/3, p256* The restaurant turns into a noisy bar late at night. Seats spill out onto the square. Backpackers and students favourite.

Elle 51, 51 Plein St, **T** 021-8839525. *Map 8, E2/3, p256* Breezy and stylish bar serving snacks and drinks to yuppies and trendy students.

Fandango, 25 Bird St, **T** 021-8877506. *1000-late. Map 8, E2/3, p256* Café and bar offering internet, tables on square.

Finlay's Wine Bar, Plein St, **T** 021-8866066. *1130-late. Map 8, E2/3, p256* A lively long bar with a few tables for quick meals served from the back, buzzing at lunch and after work, large selection of wines, popular with the yuppie crowd, prices above average, friendly service.

Live, Adringa St. *Map 8, E2/3, p256* Popular student hangout, bar and club.

Mavericks, corner Bird and Plein sts. *Map 8, E2/3, p256* Bar and club, another popular student haunt.

O'Hagans, 43 Bird St, **T** 021-7881135. *1100-late. Map 8, E2/3, p256* Irish theme pub, part of a chain which serves generous pub meals, good range of beers including imported (check sell by dates – they don't move fast on account of the price), popular most nights, a serious drinking haunt with food.

Stones, Bird St, **T** 021-3871942. *1100-late. Map 8, E2/3, p256* Lively bar and pool hall, plenty of tables, seats on outdoor balcony overlooking the street, very popular, gets packed and noisy later in the night.

The Terrace, The Terrace, Alexander St, **T** 021-3871942. *1200-1500, 1830-late. Map 8, E2/3, p256* Busy pub with outdoor tables overlooking the Braak, live music most nights.

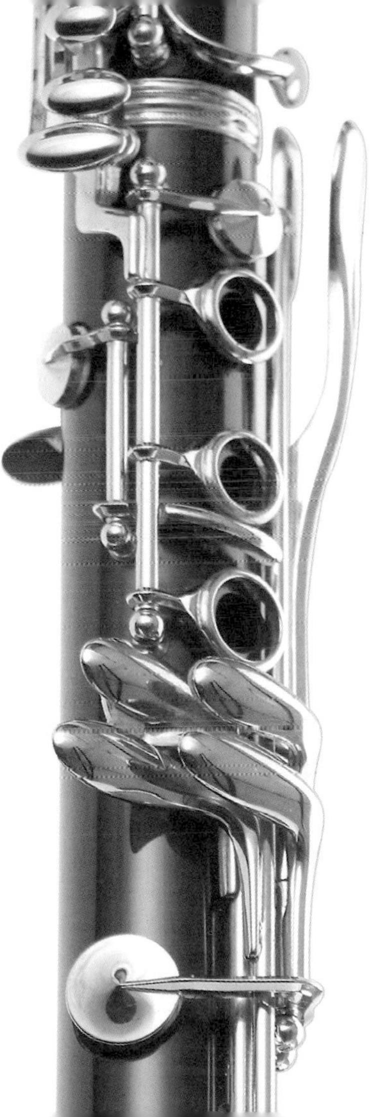

Arts and entertainment

Following fast in Jo'Burg's footsteps, Cape Town is gaining a solid reputation for having a vibrant arts scene. Music, as always, is the cultural focal point, with live music – particularly jazz – remaining hugely popular and culminating in the yearly North Sea Jazz Festival, see also p185. The comedy circuit, too, is booming, attracting talent from around South Africa and overseas. The city also prides itself on its well-established classical music, opera and dance companies, although these have started to modernize in recent years – the staid, whites-only scene is becoming more inclusive and experimental (and therefore much more interesting). Modern dance and theatre remain popular, although much of the fodder for political theatre, once the most fertile genre in the performing arts, has disappeared. Instead, large-scale musicals have become the most popular productions.

Computicket: www.computicket.com, T083-9158000, for nationwide theatre, concerts and sport events.

Cinema

Despite Cape Town's major role as a film location – the city and its surrounds have acted as stand-ins for an impressive range of films in recent years – there is very little in the way of local cinema. Instead, cinemas tend to screen Hollywood blockbusters and mainstream releases.

The two major cinema groups are **Nu Metro** and **Ster-Kinekor**, both of which have several modern multi-plexes dotted around the city. Some of the Ster-Kinekor multi-plexes (V & A Waterfront and Cavendish Square) have an attached Cinema Nouveau, concentrating on foreign and art-house cinema. There are also a couple of Independent cinemas which screen international and art-house releases.

New films are released on Friday. Evening and weekend shows are very popular so booking ahead is a good idea. Daily newspapers and the monthly *Cape Review* have full listings.

Nu Metro, V & A Waterfront, **T** 021-4199700. *Map 3, B11, p251* 11 screens, usually about R15-20 entry, large, modern complex with usual snacks on offer, roomy air-conditioned cinemas, block-busters and new releases; Century City, **T** 021-5552510. Huge complex popular with families; Claremont, **T** 021-6831122. *Map 1, C4, p246*. Similar set-up with plenty of screens showing latest releases, gets very busy at weekends and Tuesdays when tickets are half-price.

Ster-Kinekor, Golden Acre, Adderley St, **T** 021-9395126. *Map 2, A9, p249*. Plenty of choice plus range of snacks on offer, cheap nights on Tuesdays; Cavendish Sq, **T** 021-6836238. *Map 3, H11, p251*. Number of screens, usual multiplex set-up, most shows get sold out on Fridays and Saturdays; Kenilworth, **T** 021-6831208/9. Slightly smaller, but good choice and same facilities and services on offer.

Baxter, Main Rd, Rondebosch, **T** 021-6891069. *R20-40. Map 1, C4, p246* Two screens, part of the theatre complex, art-house and foreign-language films, arty sophisticated crowd, around R20.

Labia, 68 Orange St, Gardens, **T** 021-4245927, labia@new.co.za *R20-60. Map 2, D5, p248* Two screens, international art house films, trendy crowd, some good South African cinema, tickets around R20.

Imax cinema, in the BMW Pavilion at the V & A Waterfront, **T** 021-4197365. *Map 3, B10, p251* Shows special format films on a giant screen with 'six-channel wrap-around digital sound'. Check the papers for listings of what's on. Tickets cost approximately R50 for adults and each film lasts for one hour.

Comedy

The comedy circuit is booming in Cape Town, led by the Cape Comedy Collective, a group of comedians who tour the city hosting nights at different venues. The scene is very cutting edge, playing on the multitude of issues that plague modern South Africa – not for the easily offended. It is also perhaps the most mixed scene in the city, both in terms of comedians and audiences, a welcome change from the often still-segregated nightlife scene. Comedians come and go at break-neck speed, but some of the most popular at time of writing include well-established Marc Lottering and the up-and-coming Kurt Schoonraad, from Mitchell's Plain on the Cape Flats. Stand up shows, the best of which are on weekends (including Sunday night) are almost always excellent, offering a hilarious and thought-provoking insight to the city – providing not too many of the punch lines are in Afrikaans. For listings and information check the *Cape Times* or visit www.comedyclub.co.za

Bijou, Lower Main Rd, Observatory, **T** 021-4480183. *Tue-Sun 2000-late. Map 7, A3, p255* Ultra-fashionable club/bar/open-air theatre. Hosts some of the stand-up comedians visiting Cape Town for the annual Smirnoff Comedy Festival, held in October.

Comedy Warehouse, 55 Somerset Rd, Green Point, **T** 021-4252175. *2000-late. Map 3, F10, 251* Stand up comedy on Friday and Saturday, also hosts Smirnoff Sessions and Cape Comedy Collective.

Independent Armchair Theatre, 135 Lower Main Rd, Observatory, **T** 021-4471514. *Daily 2000-0100. Map 7, A3, p255* Popular venue with huge sofas to lounge in, hosts the Cape Comedy Collective on Sunday, also sometimes has open mic nights.

Dance

The dance scene is not as big as one might expect, considering Cape Town's thriving arts scene, but there are occasionally one or two shows on that are worth seeing. Ballet is no longer very prominent, but there is some interesting modern dance around, especially when it incorporates aspects of African dance. Tap-dancing, too, is making a bit of a comeback, although there's little here that can't be seen at home.

The Cape Town City Ballet, Cottage 3, Lover's Walk, Rosebank, www.capetowncityballet.org.za, **T** 021-6868807. *Map 7, H4, p255* This company has a long and illustrious history, starting with the establishment of Dulci Howes' UCT Ballet Company in 1934. Although once a large and well-funded company, it has suffered in recent years from the reallocation of government funding, and the regular large scale, big-bucks productions have been replaced with a smaller company of just 30 dancers, with performances to recorded music instead of with an accompanying orchestra. Nevertheless, they remain of a high standard, concentrating on traditional favourites such as *Giselle* and *Cinderella*.

Jazzart, Artscape Theatre Centre, DF Malan St, Foreshore, east of the train station, www.jazzart.co.za, **T** 021-4109848. The other major player in Cape Town's dance scene is the oldest modern dance company in South Africa, founded in 1975. Unlike the City Ballet, Jazzart was not granted funding during apartheid – little surprise considering its history of cultural involvement and multi-racial performances. The company continues to be actively involved in disadvantaged communities, working as a racially mixed group and creating a fusion of Western and African dance styles.

Music

Cape Jazz is perhaps Cape Town's greatest cultural gift, and if you get the chance try and see some live acts while you're here. Jazz was, and remains, an important expression of cultural trends in modern South Africa and Cape Town has produced some of its greatest exponents. The North Sea Jazz Festival, see p185, is held every March and attracts a glittering array of artists, including Erykah Badu, Hugh Masekela and Judith Sephuma in 2002. See also p230.

Classical music and opera, although only recently moving away from the realm of the white and wealthy, is becoming increasingly accessible – not least at the summer concerts held at Kirstenbosch Botanical Gardens. The Cape Town Opera, www.cape townopera. co.za, stages regular performances, with new up-and-coming singers leading the way. Cape Town also has a well-respected Philharmonic Orchestra, with concerts held at the Artscape Complex.

Rock and funk bands are big business, and are best caught at the Long Street or Obs Festivals – the controversially named band Golliwog is one of the most popular funk bands at the moment.

The Brass Bell, Kalk Bay, **T** 021-7885455. *1200-late. Map 1, G3, p247* This long-term favourite has one of the best locations on False Bay, set just above the waves with views of the Atlantic.

The bar is nothing special. Serving up cheap meals and beers to a young, surfer crowd. Music is rock and pop with live bands on weekends.

Dizzy Jazz Café, 41 The Drive, Camps Bay, **T** 021-4382686. *Mon-Fri 1700-late, Sat and Sun 1000-late, closed Tue. Map 5, E4, p253* Busy bar and live jazz, intimate venue compared to others, friendly, well-heeled crowd, good food served, very popular jazz nights at the weekend.

Drum Cafe, 32 Glyn St, Gardens, **T** 021-4611305, www.drumcafe. co.za *2000-late. Map 2, D9, p249* Popular, featuring communal drumming sessions or professionals on Friday and Saturday nights.

Green Dolphin, V & A Waterfront, **T** 021-4217471. *1200-late. Map 3, C10, p251* Best place in Cape Town to hear top quality jazz.

Independent Armchair Theatre, 135 Lower Main Rd, Observatory, **T** 021-4471514. *1800-midnight. Map 7, A3, p255* Popular venue with huge sofas to lounge in, jazz on Thursday, live bands most nights.

Kirstenbosch Summer Concerts, Kirstenbosch Botanical Gardens, www.nbi.ac.za *Every Sun at 1700 Nov to Mar. Map 1, D3, p246* Idyllic setting, picnics on the lawns, concerts varying from folk and jazz to classical and opera.

Mama Africa, 178 Long St, **T** 021-4248634. *1900-late. Map 2, B7, p249* Great live music every night, usually Marimba.

V & A Waterfront Amphitheatre, outdoor venue on the Waterfront, **T** 021-4087500. *All day and night.* *Map 3, C11, p251* With daily concerts, live performances, mainly jazz.

Theatre

Cape Town's theatre scene has suffered somewhat in recent years, largely due to the reallocation of government funds and the decline of political theatre, a pivotal genre in the Apartheid era. Cutting-edge productions are few and far between, while large-scale musicals remain the most popular form of theatre – Cats recently opened here and it is a huge success. Most mainstream performances are held at the Artscape Complex, but for more alternative productions try the Baxter Theatre, usually the most reliable venue for quality, thought-provoking performances.

Artscape, DF Malan St, Foreshore, east of the train station, **T** 021-4109800. *Matinee and evening shows.* Major complex offering opera, theatre and classical music concerts. Three-theatre complex – Main Theatre, Arena and the Opera House, musicals, dance and new experimental theatre; opera is rarely staged due to production costs.

Baxter, Main Rd, Rondebosch, **T** 021-6857880, www.baxter.co.za *Matinee and evening shows.* *Map 1, C4, p246* Long-term involvement in black theatre, good reputation for supporting community theatre, international productions and musicals.

Bijou, Lower Main Rd, Observatory, **T** 021-4480183. *Tue-Sun 2000-late.* *Map 7, A3, p255* Ultra-fashionable club/bar/open-air theatre. Weekly shows, mostly alternative theatre or live music.

Celebrations are a serious business in Cape Town, and during the summer months you'll be hard pressed to find a free weekend. The city makes the most of its beautiful setting, with most events taking place outdoors. Street carnivals and festivals compete with cultural and sporting events, although perhaps the best known event is the Karnaval in January, a street parade of competing minstrel bands. Other festivals to look out for is the young and vibey Long Street Carnival, the excellent Jazz festival held in March, and of course the famous summer concerts held at Kirstenbosch Botanical Gardens. Surprisingly, publicity is often limited and you may only hear about an event after it has taken place, but the *Cape Times* usually has good up-to-date information on what's on, or have a look at www.capetownevents.co.za The winter months are a lot quieter, although this is the best time to visit Hermanus for its superb whale watching and its Whale Festival.

January

Karnaval (2nd), popularly known as the Coon Carnival (despite its derogatory connotations), begins in the Bo-Kaap district and ends up in the Green Point Stadium. It is without doubt the city's most popular festival. The procession of competing minstrel bands, complete with painted faces, straw boaters and bright satin suits, is quite the spectacle.

Cape to Rio yacht race starts on the first weekend of January. It's held every two years, the next one is in 2004. It is a mammoth event starting in Cape Town. Much of the world's sailing fraternity comes here – accommodation gets booked up months in advance.

J&B Metropolitan Handicap, held on the last Saturday of the month, is South Africa's major horse-racing meet at Kenilworth Race Course. See www.jbmet.co.za for further information.

March

African Harvest North Sea Jazz Festival is held on the last weekend of the month. This is the second leg of the North Sea festival (held in the Hague) and is the city's biggest annual jazz event. Held in the Good Hope Centre, there are usually four stages featuring a weekend's worth of local and international jazz artists, from local talent to international big names like Erika Badu. For more information, see www.nsjfcapetown.com

Cape Argus Pick 'n' Pay Cycle Tour is also held on a Saturday in this month and is the world's largest timed cycling event. The tour follows a gruelling circuit around Table Mountain to False Bay, then across the mountains to the Atlantic Seaboard and heads back into the centre of town. Much of the city is out of bounds to motorists for the day. See also www.cycletour.co.za

Two Oceans Marathon, held on the last weekend of the month, is a very popular race covering 56 km and following a similar course to the Pick 'n' Pay Cycle Tour (hence the name Two Oceans). It is similar to the London Marathon, in that there are over 9,000 competitors, many of which are running for charity, so expect the usual wacky costumes. Again, much of the city is closed to motorists. See www.twooceansmarathon.org.za

---

August

Cape Times Wine Festival takes place on the V & A Waterfront on the last weekend of the month. There are 300 wines to taste from 85 estates plus a cheese hall.

September

Hermanus Whale Festival takes place during the last week of the month and marks the beginning of calving season of Southern Right Whales. This is in essence a community festival but attracts visitors from all around the Cape. The festivities kick off with an open-air concert at the Old Harbour, and continue with theatre, comedy, live music and sporting events (including a mini-marathon) held throughout the week. See www.whalefestival.co.za

---

October

Cape Times/FNB Big Walk takes place on a weekend in the middle of the month. It is the world's largest timed walk, with an estimated 20,000 people taking part. The walk, marketed as a fun-walk but with a more serious, longer walk added on for sporty types, has been going on for some time, having started in 1903, and is aimed specifically at raising money for charities. See www.bigwalk.co.za for details.

Smirnoff International Comedy Festival, held at the Baxter Theatre, is a week-long festival following a similar week-long event in Johannesburg. There is a nightly Smirnoff show, featuring between five and 10 stand-up comedians, including local talent and British, American and Australian imports. The standard is generally very high, as is the demand for tickets, so be sure to book ahead. There are also a couple of individual stand-up shows at comedy venues around town.

November

Nedbank Summer Concerts are held at the Josephine Mill, Newlands, every Sunday from November through to February. A whole range of musical performances: classical, jazz, folk, swing and choral.

December

Obz Festival held on a Saturday at the beginning of the month, is a huge one-day street party held in the bohemian suburb of Observatory. The main stage is set up on Lower Main Street, and features non-stop live music from local jazz and funk bands, plus stand-up comedy and some rock music. There are also dozens of stalls selling second-hand clothes, trendy bags and jewellery, plus food and drink stands. All of the bars and cafés open their doors and hold all-night parties. The festival has a distinctly local feel, although it attracts the young and hip from all round Cape Town.

Long Street Carnival, held for a weekend in the middle of the month, is another street party, held on buzzing Long Street. Several stages are set up along the road and down some of the side streets, featuring live music (mostly rock bands and techno music) and stand-up comedy. There are also a couple of fairground rides and a number of stalls selling clothes, music and food.

Although the festival can be rather forlorn during the day, it really fills up in the evenings. See www.longstreet.co.za

Mother City Queer Project costume party, held on a Saturday night at the beginning of the month, is a vast costume party and the biggest gay event in town. Basically an all-night dance event, this is one of the best parties in Cape Town, with several stages playing techno, house, funk and 70's disco hits. The annual theme (it was Farm Fresh in 2002) guarantees outrageous and hilarious costumes and an up-beat atmosphere. The venue changes every year, but is usually held somewhere with a large capacity (such as the Good Hope Centre), and the event's huge popularity means ticket usually sell out. See www.mcqp.co.za for more details.

Clifton Challenge, on Clifton Beach 4 on a Saturday in the middle of the month, is a fitness challenge between the Springbok rugby team and local Clifton lifesavers. This is *the* event for the beautiful people, attracting the usual well-heeled beach crowd, and entails a day of tug-of-war and similar 'tests', plus live music and competitions. There is also the 'Mr and Mrs Clifton' competition, a rather archaic beauty show with inevitable bronzed blonds winning the cherished titles.

Kirstenbosch Summer Concerts take place every Sunday from December until March. These are undoubtedly a summer highlight and should not be missed. The outdoor concerts are held on rolling lawns in Kirstenbosch Botanical Gardens, with the unrivalled backdrop of the mountains and gardens. The atmosphere is typically relaxed: visitors spread blankets on the grass and enjoy boozy picnics while listening to the music. The concerts ranges from popular classics and opera to jazz, world music and South African favourites such as Johnny Clegg. See www.nbi.ac.za for more details.

Cape Town represents excellent value for money for shoppers, and many well-heeled visitors come here for little else. The Cape Times and Argus run regular gleeful stories reporting on individual tourists who spend millions of Rand in a few days' visit. While this is rather above most visitors' budgets, stocking up on curios, clothes and crafts is well worth it. The main shopping area is the V & A Waterfront, which is crammed with clothes, souvenir, music and crafts shops – but prices are a little over the average here. The city centre also has a good range, with a couple of craft markets, some excellent second-hand book, antique and bric-a-brac shops and a handful of trendy clothes shops. Capetonians stick to their trusted shopping malls, the largest and glitziest is Century City off the N1 to Belville, 15 minutes from the city centre, home also to Ratanga Junction, see Kids, p214. More accessible and not quite as overwhelming is Cavendish Square in Claremont. Most of the better clothes chains and small boutiques are in Cape Town's shopping malls. Long St and Kloof St are good bets for more alternative clothes.

Cape Town

Arts, crafts and curios

African Image, 52 Burg St, **T** 021-4238385. *0830-1700 weekdays, 0830-1300 Sat, closed Sun. Map 2, A8, p249* Not your everyday curio shop, the tribal art and crafts here are of a superior quality and could well become an investment.

Art Etc, 149 Kloof St, **T** 021-4240567. *0830-1700 weekdays, 0830-1300 Sat, closed Sun. Map 2, E3, p248* Unusual collection of art and ceramics by local artists.

Constantia Craft Market, Constantia Centre, **T** 021-5312653. *0900-1700. Map 1, D3, p246* First and last Saturday and first Sunday of every month. Known for its wooden furniture, glass and pottery.

Indaba, Pierhead, V & A Waterfront, **T** 021-4253639. *0830-1900 Mon-Sat, 0830-1700 Sun. Map 3, C11, p251* Plenty of choice, both in price and size of curio.

Red Shed, part of Victoria Wharf shopping centre. *0830-1800 Mon-Sat, 0830-1600 Sun. Map 3, B11, p251* Handful of local crafts-men, glass blowers, goods are of suspect taste.

The Collector, 52 Church St, **T** 021-4231483. *0830-1700 weekdays, 0830-1300 Sat, closed Sun. Map 2, A7, p249* Top dealer in authentic African tribal art, quality collection of pieces from all over Africa, the prices reflect the uniqueness of the stock.

Greenmarket Square Market *Daily. Map 2, A8, p249* Lively market selling crafts, textiles and clothes from across the country.

★ **Markets**

Best
- Greenmarket Square, p194
- Green Point Market, p194
- The Pan-African Market, Long Street, p192
- Church Street Market, p194
- Grand Parade Market, p194

The Pan African Market, Long St, **T** 021-4242957. *Map 2, A8, p249* Centre selling crafts from across the continent and good local crafts made from recycled material, beadwork, ceramics. Café specializing in African food.

Waterfront Craft Market, Dock St, **T** 021-4182850. *Map 3, C10, p251* Stalls selling selection of arts and crafts from around Africa.

___

Books and maps

CNA (Central News Agencies), city-wide chain. Carry a reasonable stock of guide books, glossy coffee table publications, some colourful maps, foreign newspapers and magazines.

Exclusive Books, city-wide chain. This is a more upmarket chain with branches in most shopping centres.

Clarke's Bookshop, 211 Long St, **T** 021-4235739. *0830-1700 weekdays, 0830-1300 Sat, closed Sun. Map 2, B7, p249* A mass of antiquarian, second-hand and new books. A must for any book lover.

Jeffrey Sharpe, Alfred Mall, Victoria Wharf, **T** 021-4254641. *0830-1900 Mon-Sat, 0900-1630 Sun. Map 3, C10, p251* Africana and antiquarian maps.

Shopping

The Map Studio, Unit 7, M5 Freeway Park, Maitland, **T** 021-5104311. *0830-1700 weekdays, 0830-1300 Sat, closed Sun.* Tourist maps of towns and regions as well as official survey maps.

Clothes

The larger shopping malls have some international clothing stores, such as *Guess*, *Diesel* and *Benetton*, usually stocking the same clothes as at home, but at slightly better prices. More mainstream shops such as *Gap* or *H&M* have not made it to South Africa yet. *Woolworths* is the South African equivalent of *Marks and Spencers* and stocks similar wares at lower prices.

Victoria Wharf, Victoria and Alfred Waterfront, **T** 021-4182369. *0800-2200. Map 3, B11, p251* A shopping mall particularly popular with the young and well-heeled. Units of designer and high-street clothes selling their wares marginally cheaper than can be bought from back home.

Cavendish Square, Claremont, **T** 021-6743050. *0800-2100. Map 1, C4, p246* The same kinds of clothes can be found here as can be found at the Victoria Wharf, above.

Colour Kissis, next to the Lifestyles centre at the bottom of Kloof St, **T** 021-4265223. *0830-1700 weekdays, 0830-1300 Sat, closed Sun. Map 2, C5, p248* Has trendy accessories, T-shirts and bags.

Scar, Long St. *0830-1700 weekdays, 0830-1300 Sat, closed Sun. Map 2, B7, p249* The place to head for quirky one-off designs.

Second Time Around, 196 Long St, **T** 021-4231674. *0830-1700 weekdays, 0830-1300 Sat, closed Sun. Map 2, B6, p248* Great for 1950s and 60s clothes.

The Stock Exchange, 116 Kloof St, **T** 021-4245971. *Map 2, F3, p248* Good for second-hand designer labels.

Markets

Church Street Market, between Long and Burg sts. *Mon-Sat. Map 2, A7, p249* Antiques. Most interesting pieces shown on Fridays and Saturdays.

Grand Parade Market *0800-1400, Wed and Sat. Map 2, B9, p249* A general market selling clothes, fabrics and flowers, which takes over the large parade ground in front of the old City Hall.

Greenmarket Square Market *0800-1700 Mon-Fri, 0800-1400 Sat. Map 2, A8, p249* A lively flea market on a picturesque cobbled square, formerly a fruit and vegetable market, flanked by several terrace cafés.

Green Point Market, beside Green Point stadium. *0800-1700 Sun only. Map 3, C7, p251* Good mixture of curios, plenty of buskers.

Waterfront Explorers Market, The Red Shed. *0830-1800. Map 3, D10, p251* Not as interesting as other markets, weekends only.

Music

Musica, city-wide chain. The biggest music shop chain, selling all the latest CDs, videos and DVDs, and can be found in every shopping centre and along high streets.

The African Music Store, 90a Long St, **T** 021-4260857, africanmusic@sybaweb.co.za *0830-1730 Mon-Sat. Map 2, A7, p249* The place to head to for African music. It stocks an excellent choice of albums by major Southern African artists as well as compilations and reggae. The staff are incredibly helpful and are happy to let you listen to any number of CDs before purchasing. Recommended.

Wine

Individual wine estates are the best places to buy wine, see p89-106. Most offer shipping abroad as part of their service. Although transport and taxes can be quite pricey (expect to pay from R1,000 for the transport of 12 bottles to Europe), the excellent value for money of the actual wines means that the overall cost will still be cheaper than buying the same wines at home. Larger super markets and 'bottle shops' also stock most good South African wines.

Vaughan Johnson's Wine Shop, V & A Waterfront. *0830-1900 Mon-Sat, 1000-1700 Sun. Map 3, C10, p251* Has an excellent selection and a reliable shipping service.

Jewellery

South Africa's biggest export is gold, and the world's most famous diamond company, De Beers, is based here. Jewellery is thus quite a big draw for shoppers, although designs are usually quite traditional and pieces are not as good value as one might expect. Ethnic jewellery is widely available and very popular with visitors.

Greenmarket Square Market, *0800-1700 Mon-Fri, 0800-1400 Sat. Map 2, A8, p249* The city's main flea market has a good range of African jewellery, such as glass-bead necklaces and pieces made of ostrich shell, as well as imported Asian jewellery and silver rings and necklaces sold by local designers.

The Pan African Market, Long St, **T** 021-4242957. *0830-1700 Mon-Sat. Map 2, A8, p249* Arts and crafts centre, also has a range of good value jewellery from across the continent, including beadwork and Masai necklaces.

Kirov, Upper Level, Canal Walk, Century City, 15 minutes from the centre off the N11, **T** 021-5553730, *0800-1700 Mon-Sat, 0900-1400 Sun.* Top quality award-winning designer, selling innovative pieces using expensive components (gold, diamonds, platinum). Fine pieces with an alternative twist.

Jewel Africa, 170 Buitengracht St, Bo-Kaap, **T** 021-4245141, *0830-1700 Mon-Fri, 0900-1300 Sat. Map 2, A6, p249* Africa's largest jewellery showroom with a wide range of good quality gold, silver, platinum and precious stones. Specializes in personal designs, also features Kraal Kraft – African crafts and souvenirs.

Ute Koetter, Shop 14, Alfred Mall, V & A Waterfront, **T** 021-4211039. *0830-1700 Mon-Fri, 0900-1300 Sat. Map 3, C10, p251* Traditional high-quality jewellery design, specializing in exclusive pieces – no piece is made twice. Emphasis is on diamonds, but also has some less expensive pieces. Work shop tours by prior arrangement.

Cape Town has a serious outdoors, get-fit lifestyle – the entire population seems to spend its free time jogging along the beaches, strapping itself on to bungee ropes or hiking up Table Mountain. Its equiclimate and excellent facilities make it a great destination for adventure sports – cage diving with great white sharks, sandboarding on huge dunes, kitesurfing with the notorious southeasterly wind and paragliding from the top of Lion's Head – as well as more sedate pursuits such as watching a cricket match or playing a round of golf. There are also a number of marathons and cycle races held during summer, although the most popular sport with young Capetonians remains surfing. Most of the backpacker hostels promote an impressive choice of activities. One of the best places to visit and find out about all the options on offer is a store called Adventure Village, 229 Long St, T 021-4241580, www.adventure-village.co.za

Cape Town and around

Abseiling

Abseil Africa, Table Mountain, **T** 021-4241580. *0900-1700. Map 1, C3, p246* Operates the world's highest and longest commercial abseil – 112 m down Table Mountain.

Bungee jumping

Table Mountain Cable Car, **T** 021-4245148. *By prior arrangement. Map 1, C3, p246* For true adrenaline junkies who wish to jump from the cable car. Most are along the Garden Route.

Cricket

Newlands, PO Box 23401, Claremont 7735, 161 Camp Ground Rd, Newlands, **T** 021-6836420, **F** 6834934, www.wpca.cricket.org *Map 1, C4, p246* The famous Cape Town test match ground, which despite considerable redevelopment, still has a few of the famous old oak trees and it is still possible to watch a game from a grassy bank with Table Mountain as a backdrop. The opening match of the 2003 Cricket World Cup will be held in Cape Town in March.

Fishing

The most common catches are mako shark, long fin tuna and yellowtail, but there are strict rules governing all types of fishing. The simplest way of dealing with permits and regulations is by booking through a charter company.

Big Game Fishing Safaris, 9 Daisy Way, Newlands, **T** 021-6742203, skipper@gamefish.co.za *Map 1, C4, p246* Daily

Sports

excursions on a 12-m catamaran including crayfish lunch. Specializes in tuna and swordfish fishing.

Nauticat Charters, Hout Bay Harbour, **T** 021-7907278, nauticat@mweb.co.za *Map 1, E1, p246* Game fishing and boat charters.

Waterfront Charters, V & A Waterfront, **T** 021-4180134, www.waterfrontcharters. co.za Boat charters, fishing trips.

Golf

Expect to pay green fees of around R120-200 for 18 holes. The following is a selection of the golf clubs which are open to overseas visitors. For further details contact the Western Province Golf Union, T 021-6861668, F 6861669.

Milnerton Golf Club, Bridge Rd, Milnerton, **T** 021-5521047, **F** 5515897. Length: 6,011 m, par 72. Green fees about R120. This is a true links course in the shadow of Table Mountain, watch your par when the wind blows. A popular course set between the Atlantic Ocean and a river.

Mowbray Golf Club, Ratenberg Rd, Mowbray, **T** 021-6853018, www.mowbraygolfclub.co.za *Map 1, C4, p246* One of the oldest clubs, hosts national championships, a par 74 course with plenty of trees, bunkers and water holes.

Rondebosch Golf Club, Klipfontein, Rondebosch, **T** 021-6894176, rgc@mweb.co.za *Map 1, C4, p246* A tidy course with the Black River flowing through it.

Royal Cape Golf Club, 174 Ottery Rd, Wynberg, **T** 021-7616551, **F** 7975246. *Map 1, D4, p246* Length: 6,174 m, par 74. Expect to pay about R200 for green fees. An old course which has been the venue for major professional tournaments.

Simon's Town Country Club, **T** 021-7861233. *Map 1, I3, p247*
A nine-hole, 18-tee course. It's narrow and is a real test for anyone not used to playing in very windy conditions.

Hang-gliding and paragliding

There are 29 flying sites close to the city. For details contact one of the following companies, both of which organize excursions and day trips to surrounding sites. **Cape Albatross Hang-gliding Club**, PO Box 342, Sea Point, 8000, **T** 021-4239021, or **Two Oceans Paragliding Club**, **T** 021-4248967, **T** 0834637113 (mob).

Hiking

SA Mountain Guides Association, **T** 021-4478036. Can organize personal guides.

Due South, **T** 083-2584824 (mob), www.hikesandtours.co.za, ask for John Shardlow. Organize half- and full-day walking trips up Table Mountain. Rates include transport to/from the start point for your hike, snacks and water, and a packed lunch on full-day hikes. Take note of advice given for hiking on the mountain; bad preparation can spoil a walk for yourself as well as others in your group. Expect to pay upwards of R175 per person.

Peninsula Ramblers, **T** 021-7154434, www.ramblers.co.za
Organize a variety of hikes around the peninsula, mix of relaxed rambles with picnics and strenuous hikes.

Horse riding

There are plenty of interesting riding trails around the city, and Noordhoek Beach is especially popular at sundown.

Nordhoek Beach Horse Rides, **T** 0827741191 (mob), www.horseriding.co.za *Map 1, F2, p246*

Sleepy Hollow Horse Riding, **T** 021-7892341, **T** 0832610104 (mob).

Kitesurfing

The Cape's strong winds have made it a very popular site for kitesurfing. The best spot is Dolphin Beach at Table View, north of the city centre where winds are strong and waves perfect for jumping.

Cape Sports Centre, Langebaan, **T** 0227221114, www.cape sports.co.za If you are new to the sport contact this company for advice on equipment and tuition.

Kloofing

Kloofing (canyoning) involves hiking, boulder-hopping and swimming along mountain rivers. It is very popular on and around Table Mountain.

Day Trippers, 8 Pineway, Pinelands, **T** 021-5313274, **T** 082-807-9522 (mob), www.daytrippers.co.za Active tours popular with backpackers, kloofing can be arranged as part of a trip.

Mountain biking

Contact Bikeabout, **T** 021-5547763. For equipment hire and route advice.

Downhill Adventures, **T** 021-4220388, downhill@mweb.co.za Rent out bikes and organize tours on Table Mountain, Cape Point Nature Reserve and the Winelands.

Mountain climbing

Mountain Club of South Africa, 97 Hatfield St (close to the Jewish museum), **T** 021-4653412, **F** 4618456. Good source of information on climbing in Cape Town and throughout South Africa

Rugby

Western Province Rugby Football Union ground, Boundary Rd, Newlands, T 021-6894921. International games are played here. April is the start of rugby season at Newlands.

Sailing

Regattas are regularly held in Table Bay. The following clubs are for members only, but they do accommodate visitors if they are members of an affiliated international club.

Royal Cape Yacht Club, **T** 021-4211354. Organize regattas and holds talks and social events.

False Bay Yacht Club, **T** 021-7861703. Based in Simon's Town, offers sailing and fishing trips.

Hout Bay Yacht Club, T 021-7903110. Weekly social sailing, plus training courses.

Sandboarding

Try the latest addition to board sports on sand dunes. It is not very fast and can be frustrating if you're used to snow, but it can be fun.

Downhill Adventures, T 021-4220388, downhill@mweb.co.za Organize day trips to dunes about an hour from Cape Town.

Scuba diving

The Cape waters are cold but are often very clear and good for wreck and reef diving. A number of dive companies also specialize in great white shark cage dives along the coast. Daily dive report: T 082-2346320.

Dusky Dive Academy, 33 Castle St, T 021-4261622. Beginners' instruction.

Two Ocean Divers International, 1 Central Parade, Victoria Rd, Camps Bay, **T/F** 021-7908833, www.two-oceans.co.za Full range of PADI-recognized instruction and equipment hire, as well as organized tours to the best dive sites and great white shark cage dives.

Table Bay Diving, V & A Waterfront, T 021-4198822, spero@netactive.co.za Organizes night diving, wreck dives and seal dives and sells scuba gear.

Skydiving

Cape Parachute Club, T 021-5588514. Offers tandem jumps on the West Coast.

Citrusdal Parachute Club, T 021-4625666. Organizes jumps and offers static line courses in Citrusdal.

Surfing

Surfing is a serious business in Cape Town, and there are excellent breaks catering for learners right through to experienced surf rats. Some of the best breaks are on Long Beach, Kommetjie, Noordhoek, Llandudno, Kalk Bay, Muizenberg and Bloubergstrand. Daily surf report: **T** 021-7881350.

Downhill Adventures, **T** 021-4220388, downhill@mweb.co.za Organize day and multi-day courses as well as "Secret Surf Spots" tours.

Adventure Village, **T** 021-4241580, www.adventure-village. co.za Offer good surfing advice.

Swimming

The beaches on the Atlantic Seaboard are almost always too cold to swim in – even during the hottest months, the water temperatures rarely creep above 16°C. False Bay, however, is always a good 5°C warmer, and is perfectly pleasant for a dip during summer. Additionally, a number of beaches have artificial rock pools built by the water, which, although rather murky, can be perfect for paddling children. There are some very good municipal swimming pools in Cape Town, in Newlands, Sea Point and Woodstock. All are open air and have views of the mountain.

Tennis

Green Point Lawn Tennis Club, Vlaenberg St, **T** 021-4349527. Casual popular courts.

River Club Centre, Liesbeek Parkway, Observatory, **T** 021-4486117. Friendly club, no equipment hire, book in advance.

The Western Province Tennis Association, **T** 021-6863055. Can provide details of clubs and competitions.

Windsurfing

Langebaan has the best reputation for surfable winds on the Cape; the southeasterly roars between September and April making this the windsurfing season. In March there is a Boardsailing Marathon in False Bay, while Big Bay at Blouberg is a good spot for wave-jumping. Daily windsurf report: T 082-2346324.

Windsurfari, Blouberg, **T** 082-4499819. Arranges windsurfing holidays, and offers rentals.

Cape Sports Centre, Langebaan Lagoon, **T** 022-7721114, www.capesport.co.za Extreme watersports centre based about one hour north of Cape Town.

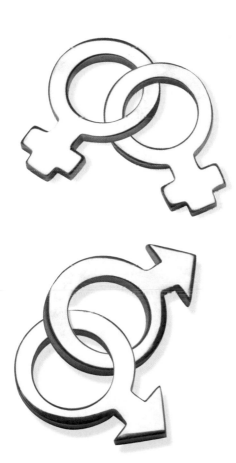

Cape Town is rated, along with Sydney and San Francisco, as one of the 'Gay Capitals' of the world. Certainly, it is the most gay- and lesbian-friendly city in Africa, with a lively scene that draws visitors from across the country and continent. There is a good range of bars, clubs and events aimed specifically at a gay crowd, many of which are the coolest in town – nights are correspondingly very popular and more mixed than you might expect.

The area around Green Point is Cape Town's gay and lesbian hotspot, and all the main bars and clubs are found along Somerset and Main Rd. The main gay event and one of the best parties of the year is the Mother City Queer Project, www.mcqp.co.za, a fantastically extravagant costume party and rave – not to be missed if you're in town in December. There is also a nationwide gay film festival, organized by Out in Africa with screenings of top gay-themed or directed films from around the world. Films are shown in Cape Town during the last two weeks of February.

An excellent guide to the gay scene is the free Pink Map, available at tourist offices and a number of trendy shops and bars around town. It has useful listings and up-to-date details of everything from bars and clubs to accommodation and steam baths.

Cape Town

Bars and clubs

A Touch of Madness, Pepper Tree Sq, Nuttal Rd, Observatory. *1500-late. Map 7, B4, p255* Flamboyant bar and restaurant run by eccentric gay couple, lavish, ironic decor, good food, great atmosphere. A pleasant alternative to the hectic scene at Green Point.

Angels, 27 Somerset Rd, Green Point, **T** 021-4198547. *Wed, Fri and Sat, 2200-late. R20. Map 3, F10, p251* Courtyard with outside bar leading on to a huge dance floor, unpretentious crowd up for a good time, house and techno plus some cheesy tunes.

Bar Code, 16 Hudson St, **T** 021-4215305. *Daily 1800-late. Map 3, G10, p252* Cape Town's only men's leather, uniform and jeans bar. Industrial interior, video, dark room, garden, serious cruising place.

Bijou, Lower Main Rd, Observatory. *2000-late Tue Sun. R15-30 after 2200 (or free with a personal invite). Map 7, A3, p255* Fashionable gay-friendly bar/club/theatre, very popular with the alternative Obs pack, weekly fashion shows, plays, gigs and parties held in a huge open-air concrete theatre on the roof, dancing area on second floor, groovy bar on ground floor, great cocktails.

Bronx, corner of Somerset Rd and Napier St, Green Point, www.bronx.co.za *Daily 1900-late. Map 3, F10, p251* Very popular gay bar, live DJs spin out thumping techno every night, gets packed out at weekends with crowds spilling onto the pavements, mostly men but women welcome.

Buena Vista Social Café, Main Rd, Green Point, **T** 021-4330611. *Daily 1200-late. R30 after 2200. Map 3, D8, p251* Ultra-trendy Cuban-themed bar and restaurant catering to a mixed, well-heeled crowd. Great Latin music, live bands at weekend, relaxed atmosphere, good but pricey cocktails.

Café Manhattan, 74 Waterkant St, Green Point, **T** 021-4216666, www.man hattan.co.za *Daily 1100-late. Map 3, F9, p251* Vibey café and restaurant serving New York-themed snacks and meals, friendly owner Russel creates a welcoming vibe.

Chilli n' Lime, 23 Somerset Rd, Green Point, **T** 082-2582382. *Daily 2100-late. R40. Map 3, F10, p251* Trendy bar and club spread over two floors, young and pretentious crowd, wild goth and S&M themed nights held on Wednesdays.

Club 55, Somerset Rd, Green Point, **T** 021-4251849, www.55. co.za *Daily 1100-late (opens 2100 on cabaret nights). R20. Map 3, F10, p251* Popular gay club, seats on pavement lead to busy dance floor inside, well-known DJs spin trance and progressive house on Fridays and Saturdays, cabaret on Tuesdays, Thursdays and Sundays.

Evita se Perron, Darling Station, Darling, 55 mins from Cape Town, **T** 022-4922831, www.evita.co.za *From R10.* Evita is a South African gay institution, a sort of Afrikaans Dame Edna, hosting lively events at her café-theatre, including Bambi's Berlin Bar, a shop, restaurant and gallery.

Jo'burg, 218 Long St, **T** 021-4220241. *Daily 1500-0300. Map 2, B6, p248* Popular bar serving pints and cocktails to a mixed crowd, gay-friendly, pool table, dance room, gets very busy at weekends, funky house and drum 'n' bass.

On Broadway, 21 Somerset Rd, Green Point, **T** 021-4188338. *2000-late. Map 3, F10, p251* Cabaret and live music venue, popular and big-name drag shows held, usually on Wednesdays, Fridays and Saturdays, meals served.

S.K.Y, Napier St, Green Point, **T** 021-4198547. *2100-late Fri and Sat. R30. Map 3, F10, p251* Fashionable dance complex, industrial interior, two dance floors, four bars, courtyard with outside bar, mixed crowd, mostly techno and progressive house.

Tour operators

Cedarberg Southern African Travel, **T** 021-4822444, info@pinkroute.co.za Tour operator using gay-owned and gay-friendly accommodation, organizes trips along the 'Pink Route'.

Strata Tours, **T** 083-3024492, stratatours@freemail.abxa.co.za Owned by two women, tours around Cape Town and South Africa, aimed at lesbian market.

Way Out Tours, michele@oia.co.za City and nationwide tours, mainly focusing on gay events and associated with the Out in Africa film festival.

Resources

Cape Organization of Gay Sport, **T** 021-5577195. Ask for Sarel. Organizes gay-friendly sporting events and get-togethers.

GALACTTIC, **T** 021-4246445, www.galacttic.co.za Association of gay-related businesses promoting gay commerce.

Out in Africa, **T** 0214659289, www.oia.co.za   Ninth annual gay film festival.

q on line, www.q.co.za   South Africa's main gay and lesbian website with email access, chat rooms and a dating service.

Triangle Project, **T** 021-4483812/3. HIV testing, counselling and a library.

Cape Town's outdoor-friendly character makes it a great place to take kids, with plenty of sights that interest adults while keeping children busy. An added bonus is that many attractions offer free entrance or substantial reductions to children (usually under 16).

An all-time favourite must be the beach. Cape Town's beaches have the added attraction of wildlife and activities. Some of the best to head for are on False Bay. Boulders Beach is safe for swimming and has the added bonus of a large penguin population. Fish Hoek has a pleasant beach with small waves and a playground. On the Atlantic side, Camps Bay has a tidal pool and shady, grassy areas. Noordhoek is too rough for swimming, but is a great place for kite-flying or a horse ride. As well as outdoor activities, a number of the museums cater for children, with the usual interactive displays and child-friendly exhibits. There are also the high-octane attractions of Ratanga Junction, complete with hair-raising roller coasters as well as gentler rides for toddlers.

Cape Town

Table Mountain Aerial Cableway, **T** 012-424818,
www.tablemountain.co.za *0830-2100/2200 (1930 in winter). R85
for an adult return, discounts for children. Map 1, C3, p246 See also
p31* The dizzying trip to the top is one of Cape Town's highlights
and guaranteed to excite children. As you ride up the floor rotates.

South Africa Museum and Planetarium, Company's Garden,
T 021-4243330. *1000-1700. R8, children free (16 years). Planetarium presentations change every few months. Shows, Mon-Fri 1400,
Sat and Sun, 1300, 1430, late showing on Tue 2000, R10. Map 2, C6,
p248 See also p34* Although the ethnography and archaeology
sections may test their patience, the major exhibits feature extensive examples of Southern African wildlife as well as dinosaur fos-
sils and a huge whale room, complete with several full-size skeletons and a whale-song cubicle. There are also regular exhibitions
with a focus on entertaining and educating school children. The
shop has an above average selection of trinkets, games and puzzles.

Two Oceans Aquarium, Dock Rd, **T** 021-4183823, www.aquar-
ium.co.za *0930-1800. Daily feeds at 1530. R45, children R20. Map 3,
C9, p251 See also p56* This is highly recommended and very popular for families. The displays are fascinating and simply labelled.
The basement holds the Alpha Activity Centre, where free puppet
shows and face painting keep children busy. There are also touch
pools, where children can pick up spiky starfish and slimy sea slugs.
The highlight is the predators exhibit, holding ragged-tooth
sharks, eagle rays and some impressively large hunting fish.

Telekom Exploratorium, V & A Waterfront, **T** 021-4195957.
*Tue-Sun 0900-1800, R10, children R5. Map 3, C10, p251 See also
p55* This is the only museum in Cape Town targeted specifically at
children. Housed in the Union Castle Building (1919), the

exhibitions focus on technology and communication, with plenty of hands-on displays, virtual reality rides and simulators.

Ratanga Junction, Century City, **T** 021-5508500. *Wed-Fri and Sun 1000-1700, Sat 1000-1800 (extended during school holidays). Follow the N1 to Belville and take exit 10 for Century City. R75, children R39.* South Africa's largest theme park is a recreation of a 19th-century mining town, crammed with impressive thrill rides, roller coasters and family rides. Tickets allow as many rides as you want. Some have a height restriction.

Boulders Beach, **T** 021-7862329, boulders@parks-sa.co.za *0800-1700. R10, free at other times. Map 1, I3, p247 See also p83* Boulders is one of the most attractive beaches on the False Bay and also the best place for spotting African penguins. Hundreds of birds live on the beach – taking little notice of their sunbathing neighbours happily going about their business. Also an excellent swimming beach with no waves.

Kirstenbosch Botanical Gardens, **T** 021-7998783, weekends **T** 021-7998620, www.nbi.ac.za *Sep-Mar 0800-1900, Apr-Aug 0800-1800. R15, children R5. Map 1, D3, p246 See also p72* South Africa's oldest, largest and most exquisite botanical garden is the perfect spot for a family picnic. The rolling lawns and shady areas are great for toddlers to run about on, while the Fragrance garden or the Medicinal Plants garden will interest older kids. There are also plenty of hidden forest trails, perfect for playing hide and seek.

Cape of Good Hope Nature Reserve, **T** 021-7018692, www.cpnp.co.za *0600-1800 Oct-Mar, 0700-1700 Apr-Sep. R25. Map 1, K3, p247 See also p64* The nature reserve is a wonderful area to spend a day wandering and picnicking. There are some easy walks suitable for older children, and a number of deserted beaches perfect for stopping for a picnic or flying a kite.

Airline offices

Air Namibia, T 021-9362755. **Air Zimbabwe**, T 021-9361186. **British Airways**, T 0806-0011747. **Comair**, T 021-9369000. **Egypt Air**, T 021-4618056. **KLM**, Main Tower, Standard Bank Centre, T 021-4211870, T 021-9343495, F 4182712. **Lufthansa**, T 4153535, T 021-9348534, F 9345063. **Malaysia Airlines**, Safmarine House, 22 Riebeeck St, T 021-4198010. **National Airlines**, T 021-9340350, F 9343373. **Olympic Airways**, 22 Riebeeck St, T 021-4192502, F 4211199. **Singapore Airlines**, 21 Dreyer St, Claremont, T 021-6740601, F 6740710. **South African Airways**, Southern Life Centre, 8 Riebeeck St, reservations T 021-9361111, F 4055944. **Swissair**, T 021-9348101.

Banks and ATMs

Only as a last resort change money in hotels as their exchange rates are unbelievably poor. There are plenty of 24-hour cash machines (ATMs) throughout the city, making it easy to keep in funds. There are also a number of banks where you can cash traveller's cheques. All the main branches are open weekdays 0830-1530 and Sat 0800-1100. The following are the principal branches in Cape Town city centre (Adderley Street). **ABSA**, **First National Bank**, **Standard Bank**, **Trust Bank**, T 021-4234080. The main bureaux de change is **Amex**, Thibault Sq. They will receive and hold mail for card holders, open Mon to Fri 0830-1700, Sat 0900-1200. They have a second office at the Victoria and Alfred Waterfront in Alfred Mall, T 021-4193917, open until 1900 on weekdays and 1700 weekends. **Rennies Travel** (Thomas Cook representatives), 2 St George's Mall, T 021-4181206, open Mon-Fri, 0830-1700, Sat, 0900-1200, also have a branch at the Waterfront, on the upper level of Victoria Wharf, T 021-4183744. **Rennies Travel** also provides all the usual services of a travel agent.

Bicycle hire

See Sports, p203.

Car hire

Adelphi Car Rental, 94 Main Rd, Sea Point, T 021-4396144, F 4395093, adelphi@intekom.co.za **Atlantic Car Hire**, T 021-9344600, F 9344549, T 082-9004278 (mob). **Avis**, 123 Strand St, T 021-4241177, F 4233601, T 0800-021111, www.avis.com **Best Boland Motors**, T 021-9814113, original VW Beetles. **Brights**, 13 Foregate Sq, T 021-4252687, Foreshore. Good value small company. **Budget**, 63 Strand St, T 0860-016622, www.budget.com **Cape Car Hire**, 217 Lansdowne Rd, Claremont, T 021-6832441, F 6832443, www.capecarhire.co.za **Europcar**, 33 Heerengracht, Foreshore, T 021-4180670, F 4180609. **Hertz**, 371 Main Rd, Sea Point, T 021-4391144, F 4394031, T 0800-600136, www.hertz.com **Imperial**, Strand St, T 021-4215190, F 4252382, T 0800-131000. The following companies have a kiosk in one of the airport terminals. Their main offices and depot are to the left when you exit the arrivals building. **Avis**, T 021-9340330, www.avis.com **Budget**, T 021-9340216, F 9340151. **Europcar**, T 021-9342263, F 9346620. **Hertz**, T 021-4221515, F 4221703. **Imperial**, T 021-3863239, F 3863240. **Tempest**, T 021-9343845, F 9343853.

Credit card line

Stolen credit cards: T 809534300.

Cultural institutions

British Council, T 021-4606660, www.britishcouncil.org/southafrica; **Iziko Museums of Cape Town**, www.museums.org.za/iziko; **University of Cape Town**, www.uct.ac.za; **South Africa Cultural Heritage**, www.saculturalheritage.org; **South African History**, www.sahistory.org.za

Dentists

Cape Town Dental Clinic, T 021-4654017; **Med Pages**, list of health care practitioners, T 021-4181474.

Electricity

Runs on 220/230V, 50hz AC. Sockets are unique round-pinned three-pronged plugs. Plug converters can be bought in electric goods shops and Clicks. Most hotel rooms have 110 volt outlets for electric shavers.

Embassies

Most foreign representatives have their head offices in either Pretoria or Johannesburg, but many countries also have representatives in Cape Town and Port Elizabeth. **Australia**, 14th Floor, BP Centre, Thibault Sq, T 021-4195425. **Belgium**, Vogue House, Thibault Sq, T 021-4194690. **Canada**, Reserve Bank Building, 30 Hout St, T 021-4235240. **Denmark**, Southern Life Centre, Riebeeck St, T 021-4196936. **Finland**, Lincoln Rd, Oranjezicht, T 021-4614732. **France**, 2 Dean St Gardens, T 021-4231575. **Germany**, 825 St Martini Gardens, Queen Victoria St, T 021-4242410. **India**, The Terraces, 34 Bree St, T 021-4198110. **Israel**, Church Square House, Plein St, T 021-4657205. **Italy**, 2 Greys Pass, Gardens, T 021-4241256. **Japan**, Main Tower, Standard Bank Centre, Heerengracht, T 021-4251695. **Moçambique**, 45 Castle St, T4262944, visas issued within 24 hrs. **Namibia**, Main Tower, Standard Bank Building, corner of Adderley St and Hertzog Blvd, T 021-4193190. **Netherlands**, 100 Strand St, T 021-4215660. **Portugal**, Standard Bank Centre, Hertzog Blvd, T 021-4180080. **Russian Federation**, Southern Live Centre, Hertzog Blvd, T 021 4183656. **Spain**, 37 Short Market St, T 021-4222415. **Sweden**, 10th floor, Southern Life Centre, 8 Riebeeck St, T 021-4253988. **Switzerland**, 1 Thibault St, Long St, T 021-4183669. **UK**, Southern Life Centre, 8 Riebeeck St, T 021-4617220. **USA**, 4th floor, Broadway Ind Centre, Heerengracht, T 021-4214280. **Zimbabwe**, 55c Kuyper St, T 021-4614710.

Emergency numbers
Police: T10111. **Tourist Assistance Police Unit**: T4182852/3.
Ambulance: T 10177. **Mountain rescue**: T 10111. **Sea rescue**:
T 4493500. **AIDS Counselling**: T 4003400. **Citizen's Advice
Bureau**: T 4617218.

Hospitals
Casualty facilities available at: **Groot Schuur**, Observatory,
T 021-4049111, 24 hrs; **Somerset**, Green Point, T 021-4026911;
Tygerberg, Belville, T 021-9384911; **Victoria**, Wynberg,
T 021-7991111.

Internet/email
Internet access is available at backpacker hostels, Postnet branches
(see below) and at the main tourist office. **Virtual Turtle** is a
popular chain of 24-hour internet cafés, with branches at 303a
Long St, T4237508, 12 Mill St, Gardens, T4260470 and first floor
Purple Turtle building, Short Market St, T4241037. **M@in Online**,
in the Lifestyles centre at the bottom of Kloof St, Gardens, has
plenty of computers and is fairly new so has low rates. There are
also internet cafés in all the shopping centres, including Victoria
Wharf at the Waterfront.

Left luggage
There is a left-luggage facility at the train station on Adderely St
next to Platform 24.

Libraries
The main library is the **South African Public Library** on Queen
Victoria St, T 021-4246320. There are also a number of local
libraries found in the suburbs to which visitors can obtain
temporary membership cards.

Lost property

Check the 'lost and found' section in the classified section of the daily newspapers. Report your loss at the local police station and leave a contact telephone number and address.

Motorcycle hire

South African Motorcycle Tours, Sierra Cottage, Gemini Way, Constantia, T/F 021-7947887, www.sa-motorcycle-tours.com; **Freedom Africa Touring Club**, 97 Durban Rd, Mowbray, T 021-6857082, F6869112.

Media

Cape Town has an English morning paper, the **Cape Times**, and an evening paper, the **Argus**. Both are good sources of what's going on in the city, with daily listings and entertainment sections. There is also a daily paper in Afrikaans, **Die Burger** and **Xhosa**. As for the radio, **Radio KFM: 94.5 FM**, contemporary music, mix of old classics and new hits. **Radio Good Hope FM: 94-97 FM**, teenage pop music, current hits. **Radio Lotus: 97.8 FM**, general Indian affairs and music.

Medical services

Dentists and doctors are listed in the telephone directory under Dental or Medical Practiner or ask at your hotel reception. See also Hospitals above and Pharmacies below.

Pharmacies

Emergency pharmacies include **Cape Town Station**, Glengariff, Sea Point; **Southern Suburbs Pharmacy**, Belvedere Rd, Claremont; **Waterfront Pharmacy**, on the V & A Waterfront.

Post

The **General Post Office** is between Parliament and Plein sts by the Golden Acre shopping centre. Post restante is in the main hall, open 0800-1630, Sat 0800-1200. There is a separate entrance for parcels in Plein St. Regional Office, T 021-5905400. Post offices are found in all the suburbs close to the principal shopping centres. **Courier service**, Citi-Sprint is on 105 Strand St, T 021-4247131.

Public holidays
Jan 1 – New Years Day; Mar 21 – Human Rights Day, Good Friday, Family Day (Easter Monday); Apr 27 – Freedom Day, May 1 – Worker's Day; Jun 16 – Youth Day; Aug 9 – National Women's Day; Sep 24 – Heritage Day; Dec 16 – Day of Reconciliation; Dec 25 – Christmas Day; Dec 26 – Day of Goodwill.

Religious services
Anglican, St George's Cathedral, T 021-4247360; **Buddhist**, information line T 021-6853371; **Dutch Reformed**, information line T 021-4249131; **Jewish**, Cape Town Hebrew Congregation, T 021-4651405; **Muslim**, Muslim Judicial Council (0830-1300), T 021-6965150; **Roman Catholic**, St Mary's Cathedral, T 021-4611167.

Student organizations
ISTC, www.istc.org; **University of Cape Town**, www.uct.ac.za

Telephone
International enquiries, T 0903. **Local enquiries**, T 1023; **Weather enquiries**, T 082162. **Postnet** is a useful chain found throughout the city, usually in shopping malls. The main branch is in the Union Castle Building, 6 Hout St, T 021-4260179, F 4260078. Services include sending parcels, internet, fax sending and receiving, phonecards, passport photos. Open Mon-Fri 0830-1700, Sat 0830-1300.

Taxi
Dalhouzie Taxis, T 021-9194659/9192834. **Marine Taxis**,

T 021-4340434. **Unicab**, T 021-4481720. **Rikki taxi**,
T 021-4234888.

Time
The time difference is two hours ahead of Europe, seven hours ahead of America and eight hours behind Australia.

Toliets
Standard European-style toilets. There is a dearth of public toilets in Cape Town, although all museums, sights, and of course, bars and restaurants have public toilet facilities.

Transport enquiries
Baz Bus, 8 Rosedene Rd, Sea Point, T 021-4392323, www.bazbus.com **Blue Train**, T 021-4494020, www.bluetrain.co.za Golden Arrow, T 021-9378800. **Greyhound**, 1 Adderley St, T 021-5056363, www.greyhound.co.za **Intercape**, T 021-3804400, F3862488, www.intercape.co.za **Metrorail**, T0800-656463. **Spoornet**, T 086-0008888, www.spoornet.co.za **Translux**, T 021-4493333, T 011-7743333, www.translux.co.za

Travel agents and tour operators
Chelsea Travel, Waterloo Rd, Wynberg, T 021-7979999, F 7979908; **ITC Travel Services**, Fedsure building, 80 Strand St, T 021-4190050, F 4190065, itctravel@galileosa.co.za; **Pentravel**, Claremont, T 021-6832853; **STA Travel**, 31 Riebeeck St, T 021-4186570, F 4184689, capetown@statravel.co.za; **Sure Travel**, V & A Waterfront, T 021-4194331, F 4195259, www.suretravel.co.za **Wagon Trails**, T 27 11 9078063, www.wagontrails.co.za, offer adventure tours around Africa, to places such as Kruger Park, Victoria Falls, Okaovango Delta, Namibia and Malawi.

A sprint through history

28,000 BC	First evidence of human inhabitants in the Cape.
1 AD	Nomadic San people in area replaced by semi-nomadic Khoi groups.
1503	António de Saldanha, a Portuguese admiral, lands in Table Bay.
1503-10	Portuguese attempt bartering with Khoi, but relations remain hostile.
Late 1500s	British and Dutch mariners begin using the Cape to restock boats.
1652	Dutch attempt to settle in the Cape; Jan van Riebeeck lands in Table Bay.
Late 1600s	Dutch East India Company (Vereenigde Oost-Indische Compagnie or VOC). Expands settlement; Khoi are driven further out and first slaves imported from Indonesia and West Africa.
1679	Governor Simon van der Stel arrives in the Cape and begins rapid expansion. Soon founds settlement at Stellenbosch.
1688	French Protestant Huguenot refugees arrive in the Cape; most are moved to area around Stellenbosch to encourage wine production.
1780	Dutch fight the Xhosa at Great Fish River.
1795	France invades Holland, prompting the British to seize the Cape following the Battle of Muizenberg.
1803	Treaty of Amiens restores the Cape to the Batavian Republic of the Netherlands.

1806	British take control again with the resumption of the Anglo-French wars.
1825	Industrialization in Europe brings great changes to Cape Town. First steamship, the *Enterprise,* arrives in Table Bay in October.
1836	The Dutch settlers (Boer) find British administration unfavourable. Great Trek begins as they look to the interior for land.
1860	Construction begins on Victoria & Alfred Basins.
1867	Gold found at Witwatersrand.
1899-1902	Anglo-Boer war. Boers surrender in 1902.
1910	Act of Union between British colonies and Boer republics comes into being. Issues such as dual official languages are resolved, while the matter of African political rights is sidestepped. First signs of African nationalism.
1912	First meeting of the African Native National Congress, later the African National Congress (ANC).
1913	Natives Land Act prevents blacks from owning more than 7.5% of all land.
1920s	Rise in Afrikaner nationalism.
1930s	Afrikaans takes over from Dutch as an official language.
1935	Voting rights removed from last black faction (property holders in the Western Cape).
Second World War	South Africa brought into the war by Prime Minister Jan Smuts in support of the British.

1948	National Party voted in with new racist ideology of apartheid. Racial laws such as forbidding interracial marriage begin to be passed.
1952	Start of the ANC's Defiance Campaign using Gandhian tactics of peaceful resistance.
1955	ANC draws up and adopts Freedom Charter.
1959	Pan African Congress (PAC) splits from ANC under leadership of Robert Sobukwe. Massive anti-pass law campaign is launched.
1960	Sharpville massacre, followed by nationwide (black) riots and strikes. State of Emergency declared; ANC and PAC banned.
1961	South Africa leaves the British Commonwealth and becomes a Republic. Organized armed wing of the ANC, Umkhonto we Sizwe (Spear of the Nation), is formed.
1963	Nelson Mandela jailed for life.
Early 1970s	South Africa Students Organization (SASO) formed under leadership of Steve Biko.
1976	Begin of the Soweto Uprising.
1977	Steve Biko murdered.
1982	Formation of the United Democratic Front (UDF), a union of community, church and non-governmental organizations with strong links to the ANC. UDF spearheads protest throughout the 1980s.

1985	State of Emergency declared. State-sponsored murder and torture widespread; political riots and unrest escalate.
1990	Ban lifted on ANC and PAC. Nelson Mandela freed.
1994	South Africa's first democratic elections held; Nelson Mandela sworn in as president.
Mid 1990s	Truth and Reconciliation Commission, chaired by Desmond Tutu, begins hearings designed to encourage the process of national healing. Violence escalates in KwaZulu Natal between ANC and Inkharta Freedom Party (IFP) supporters.
1996	First democratic constitution passed by the Constitutional Assembly in 1996.
1999	Mandela stands down following successful elections, and is succeeded by Thabo Mbeki.
2000-01	Mbeki continues to lead South Africa following Mandela's precedent, but comes under intense criticism due to his scepticism of the link between HIV and AIDS. Meanwhile, South Africa is identified as having one of the worlds worst AIDS endemics. JM Coetzee's *Disgrace* wins the Booker Prize.
2002	Half a million South African children are identified as AIDs orphans. Johannesburg to host the World Summit on Sustainable Development.

Music

The decade following the Second World War was the great era of jazz in South Africa, a time of significant artistic development for the country, but also a period of devastating social upheaval with the rise of apartheid.

Jazz was seen as much more than a musical style – it represented an urbanised sophistication which stood in the face of prevailing apartheid ideology. Pan-tribalist and resolutely optimistic, jazz acted as a useful vehicle for a subtle form of reaction to the draconian workings of the state. A cutting-edge Americanised culture took hold in many townships, where types of dress, language and music were adopted as the ultimate opposition to the lifestyle encouraged by the government.

South African jazz became known as Marabi, with its roots in the Maraba township in Pretoria. While much of South Africa's better-known jazz developed around Johannesburg, famously represented by the socially vital magazine *Drum*, most jazz musicians and their audiences came from similar urban backgrounds, and a different scene began to flourish in Cape Town.

Although earlier African-American music was influenced by visiting American musicians, no such jazz artists toured South Africa until the mid-1950s. Instead, inspiration was transmitted mostly through film and recorded music. Cape Town however had the added advantage of being a port, and much of the vibrant scene there is attributed to the incoming influence of American sailors.

Not only did visiting sailors bring records and movies, but some of the battleships which docked in Cape Town had jazz bands on board, and new sounds spread quickly from the docks to the townships. But Cape Town's township jazz bands were not content with merely copying what they heard – instead, they combined the sounds of American swing with African beats and improvisation, creating a unique fusion which became known as Cape Jazz.

Arguably the godfather of Cape Jazz is pianist Abdullah Ibrahim, also known as Dollar Brand. Born in Cape Town in 1934, Dollar was brought up on traditional African songs, religious music and jazz, and became a professional musician in 1949, playing with the Tuxedo Slickers and Willie Max Big Band. In the late 1950s he joined Hugh Masekela, Jonas Gwanga and Kippie Moeketsi to become a central figure in South Africa's progressive jazz movement, which took its lead from New York-based sounds. They formed the Jazz Epistles, cut a groundbreaking record and performed to international critical acclaim at the first Cold Castle National Jazz Festival in 1960.

The heady days of the late 50s and early 60s soon came to an end however, and Cape Jazz, like so many other forms of cultural expression, was slowly being strangled by the state. Following the Sharpeville massacre, the cultural boycott, ludicrous radio restrictions and police bannings, many of the key players left South Africa, mainly for Europe and US. However, a handful of well-known artists stayed in South Africa, including the late Basil Coetzee, born in District Six and first gaining musical credit with Ibrahim. Coetzee remained in South Africa after the departure of many of his colleagues, and weathered the lean years working in a shoe factory. He was re-joined by prominent saxophonist Robbie Jansen in the early-1980s and so began a new chapter in Cape Jazz. A group of musicians, headed by Jansen and Coetzee, performed throughout the turbulent period of 1985-90, mostly at political and cultural events across the country, cementing the key role of music in the anti-apartheid struggle.

Meanwhile, exiled musicians continued to expand the genre abroad, and at the end of apartheid many of the original creators of Cape Jazz returned. The scene is once again flourishing. Old-timers such as Ibrahim and Jansen continue to dominate, although new influences, both from abroad and around South Africa, are once again changing the face of Cape Jazz. Yet its vital elements will always remain – both as a form of musical expression and cultural demonstration.

Books

Literature

South Africa has produced a number of internationally recognized and award-winning novelists. Probably the best known is **Nadine Gordimer**. Her novels include *A Guest of Honour*, *The Conservationist* (winner of the 1974 Booker Prize), *Burger's Daughter*, *July's People*, *A Sport of Nature*, *My Son's Story* and *None to Accompany Me*. Her beautifully written work tends to concentrate on the way wider political/social events impact on individual lives.

Another award-winning South African novelist is **John Coetzee**, whose novels include *Dusklands*, *In the Heart of the Country*, *Waiting for the Barbarians*, *Life & Times of Michael K*, *Age of Iron*, *Foe* and *The Master of Petersburg*. His language is stark and the atmosphere is bleak.

Bessie Head is a third widely respected South African author, though much of her work is set in Botswana where she was exiled in 1964. She wrote three novels – *When Rain Clouds Gather*, *Maru* and the semi-autobiographical *A Question of Power*, a collection of short-stories *The Collection of Treasures*, and a portrait of the Botswanan village where she lived and eventually died at the age of just 49, *Serowe, The Village of the Rain-wind*.

Andre Brink is another internationally recognized South African author who has published in both English and Afrikaans. His novels in English include *A Chain of Voices*, *The Ambassador*, *Looking on Darkness*, *Rumours of Rain*, *An Act of Terror* and *A Dry White Season* (made into a Hollywood film). Like Coetzee he has published extensively on literary criticism as well as his own fiction. All of these authors are highly recommended though their work is not always easy going – especially just about everything by Coetzee and Head's *A Question of Power*.

Tom Sharpe, a Englishman who lived in South Africa throughout the 1950s, represents a very different literary genre from all the books mentioned above. His two South African novels *Riotous*

Assembly and *Indecent Exposure* are both hilarious, especially because the absurd and grotesque situations and characters he conjures up seem eminently believable in the South African context.

Another South African novelist, representing a previous generation, is **Alan Paton**, internationally recognized and loved by many (though others find him overly sentimental). He is best known for his novel *Cry the Beloved Country* but he also published two others – *Too Late the Phalarope* and *Ah, But Your Land is Beautiful*, a collection of short stories *Debbie Go Home* and many works of non-fiction.

Another well-known South African novel is **Olive Schreiner**'s *The Story of an African Farm*. When it was first published in 1883 (under the pseudonym Ralph Iron) it received notoriety for its feminist and anti-racist message. **Rider Haggard**, who published his hugely popular *King Solomon's Mines* two years after Schreiner published *The Story of an African Farm*, covered very different subjects. The romantic theme of his novels with an African setting, such as *King Solomon's Mines* and *She*, remain popular today. They are certainly better written and more exciting than their modern counterparts of the Wilbur Smith variety.

The majority of the internationally recognized South African novelists described above are white. This does not mean, however, that there is not a tradition of novel writing amongst South Africa's African, Coloured and Indian populations. The two earliest African novelists in the country were **RRR Dhlomo**, who wrote *An African Tragedy*, first published 1928 and **Sol Plaatje**, who wrote *Mhudi*, completed in 1917 but not published until 1930. During the apartheid years, however, many Africans concentrated on more overtly political writings than novels. Some of these are outlined below.

Short stories have also been a fairly popular form of literature: interesting collections include *Hungry Flames and other Black South African Short Stories*, edited by Mbulelo Mzamane, Harlow, Longman, 1986 and *The Penguin Book of Contemporary South African Short Stories*, edited by Stephen Gray, London, Penguin, 1993.

Autobigraphy and political writing

The autobiography that has received most attention is, not surprisingly, **Nelson Mandela**'s *Long Walk to Freedom*, London, Little Brown, 1994, a fascinating, if at times heavy-going, insight to the struggle. A number of other ANC leaders have also published autobiographies, including a posthumous publication by **Joe Slovo**, *Slovo: the unfinished autobiography*, Randburg, Ravan Press, 1995. Previous generations of African leaders also published autobiographies including **ZK Matthews** *Freedom for my People: Southern Africa 1901-1968*, edited by Monica Wilson, London, Collins, 1981, and **Clements Kadalie** *My Life and the ICU: the Autobiography of a Black Trade Unionist in South Africa*, edited by Stanley Trapido, London, Cassell, 1970. Autobiographies tracing the lives of less famous South Africans include two volumes from **Ezekiel Mphahlele** *Down Second Avenue* and *Afrika my Music: an Autobiography*, Johannesburg, Ravan Press, 1984, *Bloke Modisane Blame me on History*, London, Penguin, 1990, and the highly recommended *Call me Woman* by **Ellen Kuzwayo**, London, Women's Press, 1985. There have also been a number of collections of political speeches, articles and other writing by major political figures such as **Steve Biko**'s *I Write what I Like*, edited by Aelred Stubbs, Edinburgh, Heinemann, 1987. Others have published diaries written while in prison, such as **Albie Sachs**'s *The Jail Diary of Albie Sachs*, London, Paladin, 1990. Another interesting diary is **Sol Plaatje**'s *Mafeking Diary: a Black Man's View of a White Man's War*, edited by John L Comaroff, Johannesburg, Southern Book Publishers, 1989.

History and biography

Many readers find that history comes alive more through biography than through general textbooks. Recommended and widely available biographies include: **Peter Alexander**'s biography of the South African novelist and well-known liberal Alan Paton, *Alan Paton*, (Oxford, OUP, 1994); **William Hancock**'s two volume biography of *Ian Smuts, The Sanguine Years, 1870-1919* and *The Fields of Force 1919-1950* (Cambridge, CUP, 1962 and 1968); **Richard Mendelsohn**'s biography of the businessman Sammy Marks, *Sammy Marks* (Cape Town, David Philip, 1991); **Antony Thomas**'s book on Cecil Rhodes, *Rhodes: The Face for Africa* (Johannesburg, Jonathan Ball, 1996); **Donald Woods**'s book on Steve Biko – the basis for the film 'Cry Freedom' – *Biko* (London, Paddington Press, 1978); **Ruth First**'s biography of the late 19th/early 20th-century novelist, feminist and anti-racism campaigner Olive Schreiner, *Olive Schreiner* (London, Women's Press, 1989); and finally **Brian Willan** on Sol Plaatje, the novelist and early African nationalist, *Sol Plaatje: South African Nationalist 1876-1932* (London, Heinemann, 1984). Biography tends to be associated with the lives of 'great men': one that is not is **Charles Van Onselen**'s *The Seed is Mine: the Life of Kas Maine, a South African Sharecropper, 1894-1985* (Oxford, James Curry,1996) – it is a long book but fascinating and highly recommended.

Natural history and environment
Good guides to game parks, wildlife and natural history include: **Jean Dorst** and **Pierre Dandelot** *A Field Guide to the Larger Mammals of Africa* (London, Collins); **Gordon Maclean Roberts**' *Birds of South Africa* (Cape Town, CTP); **CW Mackworth-Praed** and **CHB Grant** *Birds of the Southern third of Africa* (London, Longman, 1963) and **Eve Palmer** *Field Guide to the Trees of Southern Africa* (London, Collins, 1977). Three general books on the South African environment and environmental problems are: **Mamphela Ramphela** (ed) *Restoring the Land* (London, Panos, 1991), **Jacklyn Cock and Eddie Koch** (eds.) *Going Green: People, Politics and the Environment in South Africa* (Cape Town, OUP, 1991) and **Munyaradzi Chenje and Phyllis Johnson** (eds) *State of the Environment in Southern Africa* (Harare, SARDC, 1994).

Background

Language

There are 11 official languages in South Africa. Throughout the country English is widely spoken and understood. About 60% of white South Africans, and most of the coloured community in Cape Town, speak Afrikaans. The majority of black South Africans in Cape Town speak Xhosa. You will find that most people are bilingual, and road signs, for example, alternate between being in Afrikaans and English. There are a few pockets where only Afrikaans is spoken, but people should understand enough English to meet your needs. Nevertheless, it is always worth making the effort to learn a few words of Afrikaans or Xhosa – people are generally delighted that you've made the effort.

English	Afrikaans	Xhosa
how are you?	hoe gaan dit?	kunjani?
please	asseblief	nceda
thank you	dankie	enkosi
yes	ja	ewe
no	nee	hayi
excuse me	verskoon my	uxolo

braai	South African equivalent of a barbecue
burg	a term referring to a borough
dorp	a small country settlement where a road crosses a dry river bed
rooinek	literally 'redneck', a disparaging term used to describe English-speaking white South Africans
Vlei	low lying lake or swamp

Index

Bold number denotes main entry

Credits

Footprint credits
Text editor: Stephanie Lambe
Series editor: Rachel Fielding

Production: Jo Morgan, Mark Thomas
In-house cartography: Claire Benison,
Kevin Feeney, Robert Lunn,
Sarah Sorensen
Proof-reading: Elizabeth Barrick

Design: Mytton Williams
Maps: adapted from original cartography
by Netmaps SA, Barcelona, Spain

Photography credits
Front cover: Robert Harding
Inside: Francisca Kellett, Struik
Generic images: John Matchett
Back cover: Struik

Print
Manufactured in Italy by Rotolito
Lombarda, Italy

Publishing information
Footprint Cape Town
1st edition
Text and maps © Footprint Handbooks
Ltd November 2002

ISBN 1 903471 48 6
CIP DATA: a catalogue record for this
book is available from the British Library

® Footprint Handbooks and the Footprint
mark are a registered trademark of
Footprint Handbooks Ltd

Published by Footprint Handbooks
6 Riverside Court
Lower Bristol Road
Bath, BA2 3DZ, UK
T +44 (0)1225 469141
F +44 (0)1225 469461
E discover@footprintbooks.com
W www.footprintbooks.com

Distributed in the USA by
Publishers Group West

Acknowledgements

First and foremost, I'd like to thank Hugo Rifkind for his support and unwavering good humour during our travels. Not only was he uncomplaining of our hectic schedule during what was meant to be his holiday, he was an amazing help, both with research on the road and dealing with the dreaded maps.

Thank you also to everyone at 3 Fairfield Road for making living in Cape Town what it was, especially Robert Dersely for introducing me to braais and the finer details of the city's nightlife, and the German doctors for dragging me up Lion's Head. I'd also like to thank my parents and brother Dan for letting me show off Cape Town, and Jess Lipson, Laura Ferguson, Caroline Wright and Jessie Hewitson for helping me explore the more enjoyable aspects of the Winelands.

During my time in Cape Town I was assisted by an extraordinary number of people, without whom my job would have been impossible. I'm particularly indebted to SATOUR, Iziko Museums Cape Town, the Two Oceans Aquarium, and the staff at the Overseas Visitors Club, Ashanti Lodge, Oak Lodge and Long Street Backpackers. Thanks also to Lizzie Williams for her crucial last-minute work on the maps – we would have been stuck without her.

Complete title list

(P) denotes pocket
Handbook

For a different view…
choose a Footprint

Over 80 Footprint travel guides
Covering more than 145 of the world's most exciting
countries and cities in Latin America, the Caribbean, Africa, Indian
sub-continent, Australasia, North America, Southeast Asia, the
Middle East and Europe.

Discover so much more…
The finest writers. In-depth knowledge. Entertaining and accessible.
Critical restaurant and hotels reviews. Lively descriptions of all the
attractions. Get away from the crowds.

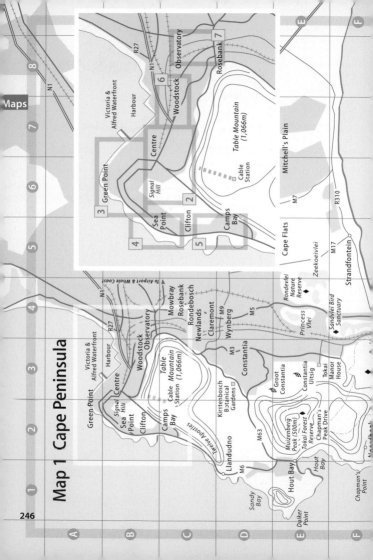

Map 1 Cape Peninsula

246

Inset (Central Cape Town):

R27
N1
Victoria & Alfred Waterfront
Harbour
6 Woodstock
Observatory
Rosebank 7
Centre
Green Point 3
Signal Hill
2
Sea Point 4
Clifton
Camps Bay 5
Table Mountain (1,066m)
Cable Station
Mitchell's Plain
Cape Flats
M7
R310
Zeekoeivlei
M17
Strandfontein

Main map:

To Airport & Whale Coast
N1
N1
R27
Victoria & Alfred Waterfront
Harbour
Centre
Green Point
Signal Hill
Sea Point
Clifton
Camps Bay
Woodstock
Observatory
Mowbray
Rosebank
Rondebosch
Newlands
Claremont
Wynberg
M9
M5
Rondevlei Nature Reserve
Princess Vlei
Sandvlei Bird Sanctuary
M3
Constantia
Table Mountain (1,066m)
Cable Station
Twelve Apostles
Kirstenbosch Botanical Gardens
Groot Constantia
Constantia Uitsig
Tokai
Tokai Manor House
Llandudno
M6
M63
Muizenberg Peak (500m)
Tokai Forest Reserve
Chapman's Peak Drive
Hout Bay
Hout Bay
Sandy Bay
Duiker Point
Chapman's Point

Map symbols

🚑 Hospital
✉ Post office
✝ Cathedral, church
🏛 Museum
ℹ Tourist information
🍇 Winery
◆ Nature reserve
⛳ Golf
⚓ Shipwreck
Related map
Detail map

N

0 km   2
0 miles   2

G   H   I   J   K   L

1   2   3   4   5   6   7   8

False Bay

St James
Kalk Bay
Clovelly
Fish Hoek
Glencairn
Shelley Beach
Simon's Town
Boulders Beach
Miller's Point
Lagoon
Valley
Ocean View
Kommetjie
Red Hill
M65
M4
Scarborough
Cape of Good Hope Nature Reserve
Olifants Bay
Thomas T Tucker
Mast Bay
Nollotu
Phyllisia
Diaz Monument
Cape of Good Hope
Buffels Bay
Tania
Lighthouse
Cape Point
Diaz Beach

Atlantic Ocean

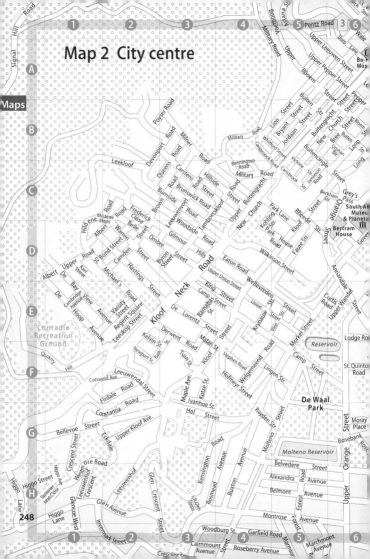

Map 2 City centre

248

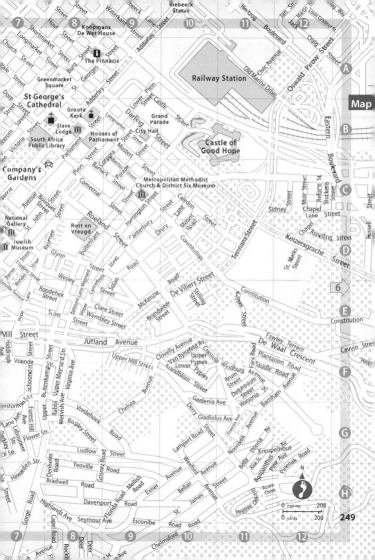

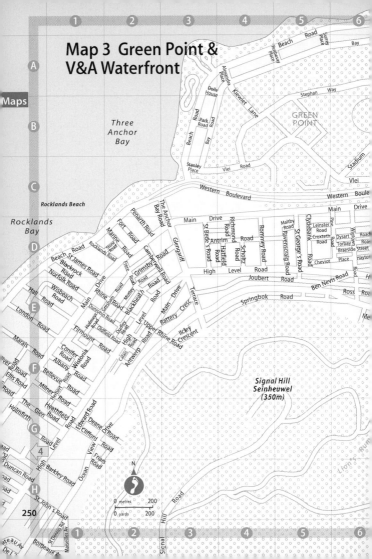

Map 3 Green Point & V&A Waterfront

Three Anchor Bay

GREEN POINT

Rocklands Beach

Rocklands Bay

Western Boulevard

Western Boule

Main Drive

Beach Road
Surrey Place
Bay

Alexandra Place

Kiewiet Lane

Stephan Way

Dolls House

Park Road

Beach Road

Bay

Stanley Place

Vlei Road

Stadium

Vlei

The Anchor Bay Road

Penarth Road

Fort Road

Main Drive

Richmond Road

Antrim Road

Rommel Road

Scholtz Road

Ravenscraig Road

St George's Road

Clydebank Road

Maltby Road

Leinster Road

Croxteth Road

Dysart Road

Wigtown Road

Torbay Road

Braeside Street

Cheviot Place

Hayton

Beach St James Road

Marine Road

Rocklands Road

Frere Road

Glengariff

St Bede's Road

Hatfield Road

High Level Road

Joubert Road

Ben Nevis Road

Ross

Me

Blackrock Road

Norfolk Road

Wisbech Road

Hall Road

Main Drive

Rhine Road

Dunrobin Road

Grimsby Road

Blackheath Road

Milner Road

Terrace

Springbok Road

London Road

Firmount Road

Hofmeyr Road

Oldfield Road

High Level Road

Battery Road

Upper Rhine Road

Ilcley Cresent

Marais Road

Conifer Road

Westonia Road

Albany Road

Dudley Road

Main Drive

Calais Road

Bellevue Road

Milner Road

Heathfield Road

Antwerp Road

Upper Rhine Road

Signal Hill
Seinheuwel
(350m)

The Glen

Holmfirth

Edward Road

Deane Drive

Clifford Road

Frere Road

Road Level

Ocean View Road

Hill Barkley Road

Signal Hill Road

Lion's Rum

250

0 metres 200
0 yards 200

St John's Road

Bordeaux Av

St Denis Rd

Marseilles Av

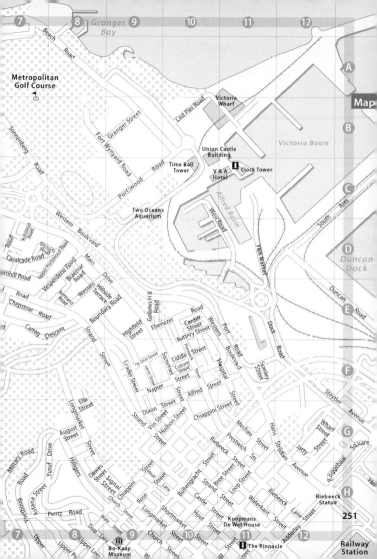

Map 4 Sea Point

Rocklands Bay

Atlantic Ocean

Graaffs' Pool

N

0 metres   200
0 yards   200

Beach s
Blac
Norfolk R
Wisbeal
Road
Hall
Road
Aurora
Lane
London   Road

Marais   Road
Cor
Albany
Bellevue
Oliver   Road
Milner
Milton   Road
Ellis   Road
The   Glen
Worcester   Road
Graham   Road
Heathfield
Road
Holmfirth   Road

Arthur's   Road
High   Level   Barkley Ro

St.   Main   Road
John's   Red   Road
Duncan Road
Irwinton   Road
Gorleston   Road
St. John's Road
Church Road
Clarens Road
Algakirk Road
Francais Avenue
Monastery
Road
St Dennis R
Beach   Road
Surf Street
St.
Andrews
Road
Casells
Road
Regent
Upper   Road
Hanover   Road
Marseilles R
Bordeaux Avenue
Quanok   Road
Kei Apple Road
Kei Apple Grove
Quendino Road
Avenue
Chateau Av
De L'Hermite Avenue
Solomons   Road
Normandie
Road
Disandt
Le Longueville Avenue
Sueur
Level   Avenue
Avenue

Alexander Road
Kings   Road
Knol
Des
Le
High
Charles   Avenue
Avenue
Disandt
Queens
Road
Huguenots
Fresnaye
Protea   Avenue
Avenue
Alexander
Park
Rochester Road
Portman
Road
La
Croix
St Patrick
Road
Princess
Avenue
St.
Louis
Avenue
A De Berrange
Avenue
Bartholomew   Avenue
Craigrownie
Saunders   Road
Fir
Ave
Banry
Lane
Alexandra
Avenue
Deauville Av.
Seacliffe Road
Brompton Ave
Bellwood Road
Brittany Avenue
St.
Charmante
Avenue
Victoria   Road
Florida
Steps
Ravine
Marina Av.
St. Jeans Av.
De Wet Road
Ocean View Drive
St. Clair Avenue
Gordon St.
Ocean View Drive
Arcadia   Road
To
Road
Leon
De Wet Road

Saunders
Rock/-rots

252

Map 5 Camps Bay

3 St Beach

CLIFTON

4 St Beach

chelor's
ve

der's
e

Victoria Road

Lower Kloof Road

Clifton Road

Lower Kloof Road

Crescent

Fishermans
Rock/-rots

Camps Bay

Whale Rock/-rots

Childworth Road

The Grange Road

Strathmore Lane

Berkley Road

Sedgemoor Road

Eldon Road

Argyle Street

Lincoln Street

The Meadows

The Chevrons

Kenilwort

Shanklin

Shanklin Crescent

Cranberry Crescent

Athol Road

Comrie Road

Montana Road

Dal Ro

Geneva Drive

The Fairway

Van Kampz Street

The Meadway

Park Road

Tree Road

Quellec Road

CAMPS BAY

Geneva Drive

Camps Bay Drive

Woodhead Close

A.F. Keen Drive

The Farquhar

Central Drive

Drive

Victoria Road

Crispin Crescent

Geneva Drive

Ronald Road

Blinkwater R.

Strathmm Avenue

St Fillans Road

Upper Tree Road

Geneva Drive

Medburn Road

Woodford Road

Hely Hutchinson Avenue

Prima Avenue

Prima Avenue

Platteklip Square

Bakoven Bay
Bakovenbaai

1st Crescent

Willesden Road

Finchley Road

Dunkeld Road

Kimoull Road

Ingleside

Camps Bay Drive

Fiskaal Road

Fiskaal Road

Fiskaal Road

Fiskaal Close

Franklin Road

Horak Avenue

Revensem Road

Hely Hutchinson Avenue

N

metres   200
yards   200

Victoria Road

Houghton Road

Kloof

ove Ro

Camps Bay Drive

Avenue

253

Map

A
B
C
D
E
F
G
H

1 2 3 4 5 6

Map 6 Woodstock

Map 7 Observatory & Rosebank

Groote Schuur Drive

Groote Schuur Hospital

OBSERVATORY

MOWBRAY

Settlers Way

Union Place

ROSEBANK

University of Cape Town

Woolsack Drive

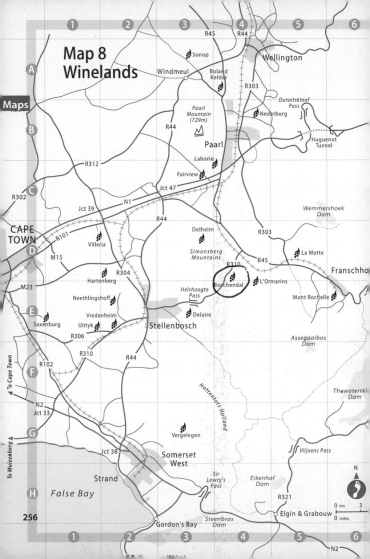